A GRASS BANK BEYOND

Fionna Carothers is the daughter of novelist Annabel Carothers. She has had very different careers from freelance fashion model to gift shop manager. In 1993 she qualified as a Blue Badge guide at Glasgow University and has worked as a guide throughout Scotland and North America.

A GRASS BANK BEYOND

Memories of Mull

Fionna Carothers

Inspired by NICHOLAS THE CAT

BIRLINN

First published in 2014 by
Birlinn Limited
West Newington House
10 Newington Road
Edinburgh
EH9 1QS

www.birlinn.co.uk

ISBN: 978 1 78027 232 0

British Library Cataloguing-in-Publication Data
A catalogue record for this book is available from the
British Library

Typeset by Iolaire Typesetting, Newtonmore
Printed and bound in Italy by Grafica Veneta
www.graficaveneta.com

INTRODUCTION

A Memory

Four ducks on a pond,
A grass bank beyond,
A blue sky of spring,
White clouds on the wing;
What a little thing
To remember for years –
To remember with tears!

William Allingham, 1824–1889

Nicholas was a cat of character and talent. Not only was he very observant, but his memoirs, *Four Ducks on a Pond*, written with the assistance of my mother, Annabel Carothers, told the story of our life on the Isle of Mull where I spent so much of my childhood. My mother, who was known as Puddy by the family, consigned the manuscript to a drawer nearly sixty years ago. I was aware of its existence, but not of its contents until curiosity led me to transfer the original manuscript to a computer. As I tapped the words onto the keyboard, they brought back a flood of memories which have inspired me to add my own.

Every family in Britain was affected by the two world wars in the first half of the twentieth century, but we were luckier than most. Our home on Mull provided the perfect refuge. Achaban House belonged to my grandparents, Grandpop and Kitten, but it lay empty because they were stranded in India at the outbreak of the Second World War. For this reason, they were unable to attend the marriage of my mother, their younger daughter, to my father. A slap-up wedding in London had been arranged but declaration of war forced a change of plan. Puddy had no experience of school outside Cheltenham. With their parents away in India, she and her elder sister Margie were sent as boarders to the Ladies' College at the end of the First World War. Poker-faced guardians and tight-laced aunts took charge during the holidays. This arrangement was not unusual at a time before air travel reduced the size of the world. Children and parents had no option but to endure long periods of separation and, as a result, Puddy attended College from the age of three, for a prodigious fifteen years. And so it was that she and Margie evacuated to Cheltenham at the outbreak of war. Apart from Mull, it was the only place they knew. And that is where she and my father were married in an intimate service among a few close friends.

After a quiet honeymoon in Devon, they settled in London and I was born a year later in a nursing home close to the Cromwell Road where a near hit in the first week of the Blitz persuaded my mother to depart with me for Mull. A cold and empty house in the middle of nowhere was a more attractive option. Despite this precaution, I nearly did not make it into the following year. A severe bout of whooping cough threatened to bring about my early demise. Following the sage advice of local people that I would be cured by the combined effects of sea air with a visit to the sacred Isle of Iona, even in the depth of winter, my mother duly bundled me up and took me across the narrow Sound of Iona and back. My speedy recovery reassured her that this advice, which might have been considered dubious – even perilous – had been worth the risk. We soon rejoined my father, who was in a reserved occupation, and therefore not in a position to leave London, and our nights were spent in the air-raid shelter beneath our block of flats. This period did not last long. Enraged by events, and being a man of action, my father enlisted with the Royal Marines, based at Chatham, while my mother and I moved to a cottage nearby.

I was three years old before I met my grandparents, Kitten and Grandpop, for the first time, and I vividly recall the day they finally arrived from India. I watched intently as my grandmother unpacked her leather dressing case, showing me each pretty item, eliciting my candid response: 'Can I have that when you're deaded?' This approach was hardly calculated to endear myself to her, but she displayed remarkable equanimity and we soon become firm friends. To me she was

Granny, but everyone called her Kitten or Pussoc, a term of endearment which derived from the Gaelic *puisaeg bhic*, meaning little cat, first used by her six elder brothers and not to be confused with Nicholas the Cat.

Kitten and Grandpop had barely met my father before he was dispatched to the Mediterranean to take part in Operation Brassard just ten days after the D-Day landings. It was a minor event with major consequences, for my father's landing craft, LCF15, was blown up and the dreaded telegram – 'missing, presumed killed' – coolly informed Puddy that she would never see her beloved husband again. Sadly I have only the vaguest recollection of my father, but he was artistic and I cherish the objects and pictures he left behind.

Grandpop and Uncle John soon became key figures in my life. Grandpop had been a doctor in the Indian Medical Service, becoming principal of the King Edward Medical College in Lahore, then in British India. John, his son and Puddy's young brother, was up at Oxford, but not for long. He joined the army and was dispatched to Italy where he saw action before he was sent home with three wound stripes. He made a full recovery and returned to Oxford but, like many of his generation, could not settle. He was a talented writer and won a national script-writing competition which took him to East Africa to work on documentary films. After a while, he decided to rejoin the army, undeterred by his previous experience, and often returned to Mull during periods of leave.

INTRODUCTION

Puddy's elder sister, Margie, was bright but imprac-
tical. She had no intention of joining the armed
services, or tilling the land, but her musical talent led
her to the headquarters of ENSA, the Entertainments
National Service Association, or Every Night Something Awful. She became continuity announcer for
Geraldo and his orchestra, visiting munitions factories
around the country, and broadcasting *Break for Music*
which was designed to boost morale for the war effort.
After the war, her boss took her with him to Ealing
Studios where she joined the casting department, and
later took charge. And it was in a pet shop close to the
studios that she first met Nicholas.

Kitten was a native of Mull. She was born in Fionnphort, directly opposite Iona, the younger of two sisters
with seven brothers. Their father was manager of the
quarry nearby, famed for its distinctive pink granite
which can be seen in the Albert Memorial, and many
prominent buildings and bridges on both sides of
the Atlantic. He had bought the old Free Kirk Manse
nearby, naming it Achaban, a contraction of the Gaelic
meaning 'white field', referring to the pale shade of
grass which grew in the field – the Big Park – beside
the house, and it was here that Kitten and Grandpop
retired upon their return from India, making a perfect
holiday home for Puddy and me.

The end of the war brought the start of my school-
ing in London and a year or so later Puddy bought
a small house in the suburbs where we could keep a

dog. Each holiday we returned to Mull, accompanied by Bruce, a black Labrador, and later Carla, a blue-roan cocker spaniel.

Like many little girls at the time, I was obsessed by horses and ballet. My lack of talent for riding or dancing did not put me off. I could make up stories in which I excelled, while reading the horsey books of Ruby Ferguson and ballet books of Noel Streatfeild. I was also absorbed by the boarding-school antics described within the beautiful plump volumes of Angela Brazil. She described a world I longed to inhabit and which Puddy enhanced by stories of her own. But the only way she, as a war widow, could finance my future education was by selling our house in London, and settling in Mull with Kitten and Grandpop.

And so it was that I spent each term away at school while Puddy gradually built up a smallholding, more out of need than desire. John and Margie came and went, sometimes for extended periods, and it was this household of three generations that Nicholas the Cat observed with a fine eye for detail. But he did not know the background to events, how they came to be, or what happened next, and this is what I intend to describe.

CHAPTER ONE

In the opening chapter of his book Nicky reported the arrival of day-old chicks on Neilachan's bus. That day in the spring of 1952 heralded a year of ups and downs, not just for the family, but for the whole community. For many years to come it would be referred to as 'the year of foot and mouth' as that dreadful disease reduced the Ross of Mull to a land devoid of sheep and cattle. This created an eerily quiet and barren landscape that took several years to recover.

Mull is second in size only to the Isle of Skye in the Inner Hebrides. It is so deeply penetrated by long sea-lochs that it is almost divided in half, the Ross of Mull with Brolass being the southern peninsula stretching towards the west where a narrow strip of sea separates it from the famous Isle of Iona. Curiously, this peninsula is a similar size and shape to Manhattan Island, but there the resemblance ends.

Achaban House is just a mile from Fionnphort where the ferry leaves for Iona, and some thirty miles from Craignure where the little boat, the *Lochinvar*, called twice daily (except Sundays) on her journey between Tobermory in the north of Mull and Oban on the mainland. The island depended almost entirely on the arrival of The Boat – as she was usually called – which carried not only passengers but all manner of cargo.

Each day she left Tobermory early in the morning and zigzagged down the Sound of Mull, stopping at Salen on the Mull side, and Lochaline on the mainland, then to Craignure before heading towards Oban. She spent two or three hours there before retracing her journey back to Tobermory. No more than four cars were carried at the most, coming aboard at Tobermory, Salen or Lochaline where there were proper piers. A pair of planks straddled the gap between pier and boat while the driver gingerly navigated the vehicle along the planks, see-sawing at the apex and then applying the brakes sharply to prevent an untimely plunge through the railings and into the sea on the opposite side. So frightening was this possibility that, so far as I am aware, it never happened.

Although there was a two-class ticket system on the *Lochinvar*, the friendly purser never issued first-class tickets, so all sections of the boat were open to all. It was like entering a club. If we did not recognise all the faces, we soon set about finding out who was who, with whom they were staying, or why they were travelling. Identification was sometimes aided by examining luggage labels: in those days few travelled with a car, so suitcases were stacked on the deck.

CHAPTER ONE

A covered enclosure was provided on the upper deck and sometimes this was sectioned off by a curtain to conceal a patient on the way to hospital in Oban, or a coffin on the way back, accompanied by grieving relatives. Livestock frequently occupied the stern of the lower deck. Sheep and cattle stood dolefully in pens, awaiting their fate with the stoic optimism of those who do not know what is going to happen next. More often than not they were on their way to Oban auction mart. On one occasion Puddy and I were travelling with Arnish, our goat, feeding her kale to keep her happy on her journey to meet a new suitor on the mainland. The boat was moving restlessly on the waves, a sure sign that we were approaching the narrow passage between Lismore Lighthouse and the Lady Rock, where the Sound of Mull meets the Firth of Lorn and the entrance to Loch Linnhe, resulting in the inevitable disturbance, even on the calmest of days, which often silenced passengers, turning them a pale shade of green. A thick fog had descended so it was somewhat disconcerting to see the sailors peering over the side of the boat, looking for a blink from the lighthouse. Puddy, ever practical, watched the radar revolving on its mast and made some comment about this useful piece of technology to one of the sailors, but he shrugged his shoulders, indicating that such new-fangled contraptions could never be trusted. The lighthouse soon loomed into sight and the hazardous rocks were narrowly avoided.

The Lady Rock acquired its name from a time long ago when a chief of the clan Maclean, having become disenchanted by his wife, saw to it that she was stranded on this small reef, knowing it would be submerged at high tide. Convinced he would never see her again, you can imagine his surprise when an invitation to dine with his father-in-law brought him face to face with his long-lost wife across the dining table. She had been rescued by a group of fishermen. He did not live to rue the day he put her there.

The *Lochinvar* was not a pretty boat. Her squat outline, stubby fake funnel and constant list to one side easily identified her at a distance from all the other boats of the MacBrayne fleet. She was built on the Clyde and launched in 1908. For nearly fifty years she toiled between Tobermory and Oban, beating the worst of storms, and reliably supplying a service which the islanders greatly appreciated.

Inevitably, she provided a great meeting point for islanders who dived down the narrow gangway and headed for the snug little bar and, beyond that, the dining saloon which occupied a space towards the bow of the ship and was therefore a rather strange angular shape. Benches against the bulkhead provided seating behind the long tables, while Sam the steward emerged from his tiny galley with huge platefuls of mince and tatties (mashed potatoes) and a long line in gossip. Above the benches a series of paintings told the story of Scott's 'young Lochinvar come out of the west' to steal his bride from the Netherby clan – a story so romantic, with pictures so evocative, that it threatened to fill developing minds with an intensely exciting idea of marriage, and weddings in particular, my own included.

There was no pier at Craignure in those days so small open motorboats met the *Lochinvar* as she wallowed in the bay, often in stormy weather. The transfer of people, goods and livestock between the boats was therefore quite hazardous. The mailbags were slung from one boat to the other, dangling from a small crane aboard the *Lochinvar*, while passengers patiently awaited the moment when the boats nudged against each other, before making the crucial leap from boat to boat, ably assisted by burly members of the crew. It was standing-room only for passengers while the mailbags were securely stacked in the bow of the motorboat as she headed for the jetty, leaving the *Lochinvar* to continue on her journey. The high hills around Craignure ensured that it was seldom dry, so passengers had to rely on waterproofs to fend off a good drenching. Occasionally it was not possible to use the jetty because the tide was too low. Undaunted, the boatmen arranged a path of planks across the rocks and guided us ashore, manhandling the less nimble to safety when necessary.

On one special occasion in 1956 the Royal Yacht *Britannia* came to Craignure. It was August – the height of summer – and the weather had been perfect only the day before, when HM The Queen and the Duke of Edinburgh visited the Isle of Iona. But a huge storm blew in during the night, and the sea was in turmoil. The royal party had been delayed during their morning visit to Oban so their arrival at Craignure was no longer assured. I had a school friend staying, so Puddy brought us to join the small crowd on the jetty, hoping to see the royal party land, but as we stood in a howling gale and pouring rain, we began to think our journey had been wasted. Then, to our amazement, we saw one of the royal barges preparing to load passengers. We watched it being winched down from the davits, and rumour had it that Prince Philip was coming ashore. It was not until the barge reached the jetty that we saw the Queen emerge, yelping as she touched the cold handrail, to be greeted by Sir Charles Maclean of Duart who was Lord Lieutenant of Argyll at the time. She was accompanied by the Duke while Princess Margaret, who had not been expected and for whom no vehicle had been provided, was crammed into the back of a small car with other members of the royal party. Peering into the car, I was caught by her amazing lavender-blue eyes which have been imprinted on my mind ever since.

The Queen and the Duke were taken to Duart Castle as guests of the Macleans, although it was too late for the lunch which had been so carefully prepared, and later the Duke drove the Queen to Tobermory for a civic reception. I know the Duke was driving, because that afternoon the three of us waited by an isolated section of the road, waving and curtsying as he and the Queen passed at considerable speed, only jamming on the brakes briefly to acknowledge us. In later years Sir Charles was elevated to the peerage and became Lord Chamberlain to the Queen's Household, an appointment which might have been kindled by this visit to Mull.

Of course days like that did not happen often – in fact they were once-in-a-lifetime events – which is why they should be recorded for posterity, as I am sure Nicholas would have done, if he had been there at the time.

Nicholas did not live long enough to know the fate of the *Lochinvar*, and perhaps that was just as well. Having faithfully plied her trade between Tobermory and Oban daily (except Sundays) for nearly fifty years, she made her final run in 1955. After five years as a relief boat, she avoided the breakers' yard by spending several years working on the Thames, where she was renamed *Anzio I* and provided a summer service between Sheerness Dockyard and Southend. A new lease of life was promised when a group of Scottish sailors offered to take her over with the intention of running a round trip between Inverness, Cromarty and Invergordon. On Friday 1st April 1966, with thirteen men on board, *Anzio I* set out into the North Sea. The sea was reasonably calm when she left Tilbury but a force 8 gale warning was predicted for the area and by Saturday a north-east gale blew up. The Lincolnshire coastguard spotted the boat heading towards land and several attempts were made to divert her but, despite their best efforts, all hands were lost as the heavy seas engulfed the little boat, shoving her ashore as nothing more than flotsam. It was a terrible tragedy and the loss was greatly felt by all those who had known the *Lochinvar* in happier times.

The name *Lochinvar* has been revived with the launch of a hybrid roll-on, roll-off ferry on the Clyde in 2013, one of only two in the world capable of using both diesel electric and lithium ion battery power. The series of paintings from the dining saloon, saved before she went to the Thames, were donated to *HMS Lochinvar* although she has since been decommissioned, while her bell and steering wheel are fittingly displayed in Duart Castle, the landmark she passed twice daily (except Sundays) during her many years of service to Mull.

CHAPTER TWO

Margie spent several nights a week at the theatre on the look-out for talent when she wasn't interviewing aspiring young artistes in her office at Ealing Studios. On her way to work, she sometimes walked past a pet shop which was near the underground station. One day her attention was drawn to a single kitten in the window. Stopping for a moment, she was caught by the irresistibly bright eyes which gazed at her through the glass. She could not help but admire the little creature's mottled fur coat with smart white front and neat black paws. Besides, she assured herself, she was about to depart for a holiday at home on Mull where a surfeit of mice would provide plenty of work for a cat.

And so it was that she set off from London with young Nicholas the Cat in a basket. Their journey would have started on Platform 14, Euston Station. On their way to the station, the taxi would pass the handsome Euston Arch, designed by Philip Hardwick and shamefully demolished in the 1960s for no better reason than it did not fit in with the station's new development.

Two sleeper trains left each evening from adjoining platforms at roughly the same time of 7.15, one bound for Perth, the other for Oban. It was easy to identify which passengers were bound for which train – the Perth ladies were coated in fur and their porters pushed trolleys laden with smart leather luggage while their gentlemen carried gun cases. Oban passengers tended to be somewhat dishevelled and accompanied by battered canvas bags and an assortment of brown paper parcels.

While the great locomotives waited patiently, belching acrid clouds of vapour into the atmosphere, passengers walked along the platform, examining the notices on each carriage which displayed their names and sleeping-berth numbers. In those days, for a reason which escapes me, tickets were divided into first and third class without a middle class, so the sleeping cars were also divided. First-class passengers could enjoy single compartments with intercommunicating doors between two if travelling together. These were well equipped with every comfort including a wash basin above a cupboard which concealed a chamber pot, neatly angled so that the contents would flow away discreetly after use. Third class provided two- and four-berth compartments with a blanket and pillow which did not require the necessity to undress, although I seem to remember we usually did, at least our outer garments.

While cats could be confined safely in a basket, dogs

were expected to travel separately in the guard's van. However, it must have been obvious by the number that arrived on the platform, and the few that travelled in the guard's van, that most were smuggled into the compartments. In the late 1940s our handsome black Labrador, Bruce, was an expert at avoiding detection. He did not have to be told to slink neatly under the bed whenever Hughie, the cheery sleeping-car attendant, knocked on the cabin door. On at least one journey three of us booked four third-class tickets, naming the occupant of the fourth bunk as Mr Bruce Carothers. But there was no doubting that Hughie knew of this subterfuge as he took three orders for morning tea in the evening, and delivered them punctually the following morning.

The train trundled steadily through the night, stopping at Crewe. A second engine was employed to drag the train over Shap Fell through the Lake District and towards Carlisle where it rested again before crossing the border into Scotland. Once more it needed to muster all its strength to climb the pass at Beattock. There was no doubting our arrival at Stirling Station, which was invariably greeted by the jaunty whistle of a porter in the days when there were porters and whistling was a tuneful art. We took advantage of the lengthy stop to take Bruce for a walk up and down the platform but, accustomed to wide open spaces, he became unduly coy and was reluctant to cock his leg without sight of a blade of grass.

Departure from Stirling, Gateway to the Highlands, was the true sign that the most spectacular part of the journey was yet to come. The single-track railway crossed the River Forth, stopping at Bridge of Allan and Dunblane before following a route past lochs and mountains, rivers and woods. Stations, strung like pearls along the line, bore lyrical names: Doune, Callander, Strathyre, Balquhidder. As its name implied, 'Bonny Strathyre' in the Pass of Leny was the prettiest, its platform graced with an elegant heron statue guarding a flowerbed encircled by pebbles. The line then climbed towards the magnificent panoramic view of Loch Earn which only the railway provided. We eagerly awaited this moment when the train skirted the hillside and the full extent of Loch Earn was revealed, making this the high point of the journey in every sense. It always fulfilled expectations.

The railway continued through Glen Ogle, clinging to the mountainside on a narrow shelf linked by a series of handsome viaducts. It was fun to watch the cars on the other side racing against the train but it was only when travelling by road that those great viaducts of the Victorian age could be truly admired. The line reached Killin Junction – with access to a branch line leading to Killin on Loch Tay – before taking a westward turn towards Crianlarich where the Callander & Oban Railway ran parallel with the West Highland Line from Glasgow, on opposite sides of Strath Fillan, accounting for the fact that there are two stations at

Tyndrum – Upper and Lower. By a sorry twist of fate the stretch of line between Stirling and Crianlarich was closed by a serious rock fall just weeks before Dr Beeching's planned cuts would have achieved the same result.

From Tyndrum the train continued through lonely Glen Lochy to Dalmally and the east side of Loch Awe with a fine view of the ruined and romantic Kilchurn Castle, a former Campbell stronghold. Loch Awe is the longest of Scotland's inland lochs, but only the broad northern end can be seen from the train as it skirts close to the shore. On the other side of the line Ben Cruachan towered above but we would not have been aware of it, just as we would not have known about the plans to gouge the rock from the heart of the mountain to create space for great turbine halls which would in due time provide Scotland with an unusual pumped storage hydro-electric scheme. When surplus power is at its cheapest, water is pumped from the loch into a man-made reservoir high on the mountain. Using gravity, and the same pipe, it is then released to power generators providing electricity for the national grid. Even when completed in the 1950s there was no evidence of all this activity within the rebranded 'Hollow Mountain'.

The train then entered the Pass of Brander, famous for a battle between King Robert the Bruce and the chief of the clan MacDougall. This road once struck terror for early motorists, but Anderson's Piano, also known as the Stone Signals, is of greater interest to rail travellers. Mr John Anderson, secretary of the Callander & Oban Railway, was concerned that the rocks high on the hillside might easily cause a nasty accident if they became dislodged and fell upon the line. He devised a signalling system whereby several parallel lines of wire formed a fence which, if struck and broken, would throw the signal to danger. His somewhat Heath Robinson system is in use to the present day. I never forgot this curious fact after hearing it for the first time aboard an observation coach which, for a brief period, was attached to the rear of the train. It offered a fantastic and intimate view of the journey, accompanied by a commentary and a simple map. The line was gaining recognition as a tourist attraction – but this enlightened approach was short-lived.

Although barely visible, it is possible to catch a glimpse of Loch Etive as the train departs from Taynuilt. Here it was that an industry flourished from 1753, not on account of the railway, which did not come until the late 1800s, but due to the surrounding woodland which provided charcoal, and the loch which gave access to the sea, allowing iron ore to be shipped in for smelting. Bonawe Iron Furnace was the most complete charcoal-fuelled ironworks in Britain and its remaining buildings are now open to the public. It was here that cannon balls which were fired during the Battle of Trafalgar were produced, and for this reason the foundry workers erected what is thought to be the first monument in Britain to commemorate Horatio, Lord Nelson. But back in the 1950s, we were unaware of this historic site when passing through Taynuilt in the train.

The next station was known as Connel Ferry although there has not been a ferry for many a year due to the construction of the handsome bridge which spans the narrow entrance to Loch Etive. Built in 1903 to carry a branch line to Ballachulish slate quarries, it was soon adapted for use by cars on an adjoining carriageway. It was too narrow to allow cars and trains to run side by side so a system like a level crossing prevented collisions. The branch line was closed in the 1960s and the rails permanently removed but the bridge continues in use by motor vehicles, one way only, guided by traffic lights. Beneath the bridge, the unusual Falls of Lora indicate the direction of the tide – by changing to either side due to a ridge of rock across the narrow entrance to Loch Etive. From flat calm, to playful eddies, and thence to turbulence, it changes throughout the day. The railway veered away from the coast at this point and disappeared into a cutting where the train waited on a short stretch of double track allowing the departing train from Oban to pass. Finally, the line circuited the southern end of Oban to make a triumphant entrance into the little town which owed its expansion to the coming of the railway in 1880.

The train from Euston usually arrived around 9 am

– just in time for breakfast – but first we needed a porter. Our favourite porter, accompanied by his dog, piled all the baggage on a painted wooden hand-barrow ready to push to the North Pier where the ferry boats left for the islands. This was on the other side of the bay while the Railway Pier, conveniently alongside the station, was used by the fishing fleet which in those days was always busy. The Mull boat – the *Lochinvar* – would not be departing until the afternoon so Margie had plenty of time to feed and water Nicholas before the next lap of the journey. A story circulated that when a MacBraynes official was asked the time of the Mull boat he replied in his gentle Highland accent, 'It's one-fifteen, but there's no telling.'

We had no need to worry about our luggage once it was on its way to the North Pier where it would be waiting for us beside the boat, so we set off across the road where Alec, the porter in the Station Hotel, would greet us warmly and usher us into the dining room. And to start the new day, what could be more delicious than a plate of plump, succulent Loch Fyne kippers for breakfast?

The first and easiest stage of the journey was over, but there was more to come before we finally reached home. The *Lochinvar* took us to Craignure Bay where we transferred by motorboat to the jetty. A two-hour drive followed, sometimes in the comfort of Florrie, our little black Ford with yellow wheels, or in the mail bus which dropped off passengers at road ends and mailbags at post offices along the way. Finally we rounded the last corner and the familiar shape of Achaban came into view. The first sight of home always raised our spirits, knowing that a warm welcome would greet us at the end of a long journey.

When Margie arrived home with Nicholas, Puddy helped with her luggage while Kitten and Grandpop stood by the front door having watched out for the bus from the study window, which had a good view of the road. Hysterical barks emanated from the house. There was no knowing how Carla would react to a new animal joining the family, so she was kept firmly behind the front door. It was a curious fact that Puddy, so down to earth and practical, owned a succession of neurotic dogs. Bruce had an unpredictable temperament which no-one took seriously until he attacked and bit Margie without any warning. Puddy had no choice but to return him to his breeder and he was replaced by Carla, a well-bred cocker spaniel, but she was more highly strung than most.

As it happens, she soon recognised that Nicholas was no threat to her, and the pair became good friends over the years, although there was no doubting who developed the upper paw.

CHAPTER THREE

The *Lochinvar* could be relied upon to make the voyage from Oban to Mull in all but the worst weather. But sometimes the worst weather came. I was once travelling to Mull with Kitten on the day before Christmas Eve and, for reasons I cannot recall, we missed the *Lochinvar*. Our only option was to board a boat bound for the Outer Hebrides which would drop us off at Tobermory on the way. But a huge storm blew in from the Atlantic. Despite its sheltered position, with the Isle of Kerrera straddled across the entrance to the bay, acting as a windbreak, the sea was in turmoil. Waves crashed over the esplanade, rain lashed and the wind howled. It was a spectacular sight, but it was clearly too hazardous to venture out even if we could. But there was no choice. The wind was sweeping against the boat, this time tied up at the Railway Pier, and she could not pull away. There was only one thing for it, and that was to spend the night on the boat and wait for the wind to calm down.

Never content to sit and do nothing, Kitten and I deposited our luggage in a cabin and then set off along

George Street, battling against the wind and aiming for the one and only form of entertainment available in Oban in those days and at that time of year: the cinema.

Now known as the Phoenix Cinema, in those days it was no more than a basic building with a corrugated-iron roof and few comforts. The fact that it was weather-proof was all we required. So we bought our tickets and settled down to watch the newsreel and 'B' movie before the main attraction began. It was not the first time we had seen *Whisky Galore!* and it would not be the last, but it was certainly the most memorable. As the story unfolded on the screen, it was hard to hear the soundtrack above the buffeting and battering of the tempest outside while the rain clattered on the roof like pins beating on a drum.

In America the film was called *Tight Little Island* because the land of prohibition banned the mention of liquor in the title. In fact the name might not have bothered them if they had known that the English title came directly from Gaelic *uisge beatha* meaning 'water of life' and *go leor* meaning 'enough' or 'plenty'. The film was made by Ealing Studios but shot on the Isle of Barra in the Outer Hebrides, and Margie was the casting director. The film owed its success in no small way to the director, Alexander Mackendrick, also of Scottish background, and the sympathetic casting of the characters who depicted island life so well – notably Gordon Jackson as the local schoolmaster and Jean

Cadell who played his primly disapproving mother. But even in the scene when the schoolmaster plays the bagpipes full burst to annoy his mother they could barely be heard above the cacophony all around us.

Kitten and I returned to the boat to find shelter in our cabin where we expected to spend the night, but quite suddenly the storm began to abate. It was decided that a smaller boat would make a special trip to Mull to ensure all passengers would be home in time for Christmas, so we transferred to the *Lochnell*, which usually worked between Oban and Lismore. So in the darkness we set off across the Firth of Lorn to be met by the bus for the long drive home.

We eagerly looked out for the bright lights of Acha-ban, which would welcome us home, but just at the road end by the school, a strange figure stopped the bus. Father Christmas came aboard carrying an empty sack. He had just delivered presents to children at the school Christmas party. The beard and red coat did not fool me. I knew it was John, who was much younger than his sisters Puddy and Margie, and more like a big brother to me. He had a short stocky build and, when not disguised as Father Christmas or Santa Claus, he always wore a kilt.

The *Lochinvar*'s timetable never varied throughout the year, but in summertime there was another option. The sleekly elegant and picturesque *King George V* sailed from Oban daily on a circumnavigation of Mull, calling at Staffa and Iona on the way. 'The Sacred Isles' cruise was very popular with tourists who had the opportunity of landing on both islands with enough time to visit Fingal's Cave and Iona Abbey. It was a trip that depended on good weather and precision timing between the *King George* and a small fleet of open motorboats which transferred the passengers – as many as 600 on a good day – between the ship and islands. Sailing from Oban, the *King George* changed her direction on alternate days, with a weekly variation to Fort William, clockwise directly to Iona or anticlockwise up the Sound of Mull, in which case she passed Tobermory and visited Staffa before arriving at Iona. The 'red boats', as they were familiarly known, were stationed at Iona and they sailed out to meet the *King George* on her arrival at Staffa before accompanying her to Iona to repeat their tendering duty all over again. It was a beautifully synchronised operation which we all took for granted. It also had a great advantage to those of us who lived in Iona or the Ross of Mull, for it avoided a tediously long and bumpy drive through Glen More on a twisty dirt-track road.

There was one problem. The train from London was due to arrive in Oban at precisely the same time that the *King George* was scheduled to depart from the North Pier. But our family had a trump card in the form of Cousin Angus, who happened to be Master of the *King George* and if he saw us coming, there was just a chance he would not budge till we were aboard.

On one occasion, as the train approached Oban, the

timing was very tight, so Puddy gave me instructions to run on ahead to hold the boat. I did exactly as she directed, sprinting from the station to the North Pier as fast as I could, with arms flailing, so worried was I that Cousin Angus would not see me. It was a beautiful day and all the passengers were hanging over the side of the ship, wondering what was causing the delay to their departure. The gangway was still down and the ropes firmly looped over the bollards when I rounded the last bend and was reassured to see Cousin Angus waving vigorously from his vantage point on the bridge.

The *King George* approached her first stop at Iona from the south of Mull and this required skilful navigation, keen judgement and sound knowledge to avoid a notorious hazard. The Torran Rocks form a reef of skerries and rocks made famous by Robert Louis Stevenson whose hero, David Balfour, was shipwrecked here during his adventures in *Kidnapped*. This was no fanciful idea of a novelist's imagination. Stevenson was well acquainted with the area, having worked with his father Thomas who designed Dubh Artach lighthouse, on the 'black rock' some miles out to sea, which gave warning of the treacherous reefs to the south and west of Iona. There was a family connection: the stone for the lighthouse came from a quarry on the Isle of Erraid, where my great-grandfather, Kitten's father, was manager. It was on this island that David Balfour arrived, not realising that at low tide he could walk across the sand to Mull.

Cousin Angus was not fazed by the fact that before the building of the lighthouse, twenty-four ships had foundered on these rocks in a single day during a great storm in 1863. He knew the western seas like few others. The *King George V* was flagship of the MacBrayne fleet and Cousin Angus was the senior captain. There was not a stone he did not know and he took great delight in steering a course through the rocks, probably more to satisfy himself than to impress his passengers, most of whom would not be aware of the peril they were in while those who knew enjoyed the thrill.

I stood on the bridge beside him, watching out for the rocks as we approached. Some were obvious, like jagged teeth, while others were smoothly rounded. Seals lay upon them like sandbags, basking in the sun, before slithering languidly into the water as we drew near. For the rocks beneath, the only indication of their menacing presence was a sinister frothing on the surface of the sea.

'It's not the ones you can see that matter,' said Cousin Angus sagely, and I have taken that as a metaphor for life ever since. In later years this carefree activity was discouraged by the powers that be long before Health and Safety came into force.

The *King George V* – also known by some as the *KGV* – had a distinguished war record. She proudly bore a plaque which recorded her service at Dunkirk when she helped evacuate troops from the beaches and miraculously escaped so many near misses that it is little wonder the Torran Rocks failed to intimidate her.

Once the Torran Rocks were safely negotiated, the shallow draft of the *King George* enabled her to advance through the Sound of Iona, the narrow gap between the isles of Iona and Mull, without stranding on the shifting sandbanks. The distinctive square tower of Iona Abbey made a prominent profile against the sky as the red boats came out to meet us. The transfer of passengers from ship to shore was carried out with well-organised efficiency. It would allow the tourists to walk up to the Abbey and back again with enough time to admire the Nunnery gardens, the Abbey Church and the ancient graveyard known as the Relig Oran.

There would be a similar landing on Staffa, allowing time to marvel at Fingal's Cave – after summoning enough courage to jump ashore. From the landing stage, steep metal steps led to a precipitous path which followed a route over a series of uneven hexagonal plates formed by the distinctive columnar basalt rock. Clinging to a rail on one side, it took about ten minutes to reach the cave, where the entrance resembled a great gothic cathedral and the columns a mighty pipe organ. The tide surged and swelled into the depth of the cave, producing the sound that inspired Felix Mendelssohn to compose his Hebrides Overture. He was not the first to notice this musical connection. The Gaelic name *An Uamh Bhin* means 'the melodious cave'.

The *King George* then followed a route round the

north of Mull. High on the headland, Glengorm Castle stood sentinel. The man who built this Disney fantasy castle adopted the name, not realising that it meant 'The Blue Glen', recalling the plumes of smoke from burning cottages at the time of the Clearances, a sad period in Mull's past which so upset Nicholas in his memoirs that he did not wish to discuss it for fear of becoming political.

The voyage could be uncomfortable in certain weather conditions. Due to her length and shallow draught, the *King George* tended to pitch and it was not unknown for passengers to turn a little pale and reach for the paper bags supplied for these occasions. Nevertheless, the 'Sacred Isles Cruise' was a very popular summer service which was not finally withdrawn until 1974.

We had done this voyage in each direction more than once. So we did not follow the tourists, but sat on the jetty at Iona with our luggage, waiting for the small ferry, painted white, and manned by Angie or Dan who would take us across the Sound to Fionnphort. A member of the family would meet us with Florrie the car for the short drive to Achaban.

On one occasion Grandpop used this route to travel home from a trip to Edinburgh. I went to the ferry to meet him. As usual there were various boxes and packages handed onto the jetty, including a neat little red bicycle. 'Would you please wheel this up to the car for me?' Grandpop said as he climbed out of the boat. 'I think it's time you learnt to ride a bicycle!' I was instructed not to attempt to ride it until after tea, and I spent an unusually long hour or so wheeling it up and down the drive until Puddy came to the rescue. I climbed into the saddle and began to pedal while she clung on to the back for all she was worth. Suddenly she let go and that little red Hercules soon became my closest companion, introducing me to a means of transport which I have enjoyed ever since.

CHAPTER FOUR

It's no exaggeration to say that my bicycle became my greatest companion, but although I was so often alone, I never felt lonely. When I was very small Grandpop called me 'Granny Tuppence' and I somehow transposed this character into an imaginary friend with a hundred children. Her eldest daughter was Susan who, unusually I think, was a very level-headed adult – and it was she who guided me throughout my formative years until one day I dispatched her to permanent exile in Australia. At other times, I was the eldest of a family that could compete with any dreamed up by Enid Blyton, although the Famous Five never appealed to me. I preferred E. Nesbit and The Wouldbegoods. I could spend hours turning circles and figures of eight on my bicycle while inventing stories in which I was the leader of the pack.

My little red bicycle also gave me the freedom of the road. The road through Mull, single-track as it still is, was rough and punctuated by puddle-filled potholes giving anything but a smooth ride, but it greatly extended my range. My desire to be pack leader remained firmly within my head – I was a risk-averse child by nature and readily accepted Puddy's strict instructions to dismount whenever a vehicle approached in either direction. This constraint was not difficult to accept because there was so little traffic. If eight cars passed the house in a day it was a talking point, so my journeys were seldom disrupted by passing vehicles.

I ventured off the main road to Kintra where a row of cottages circled a bay, or I took a bird book with me, trying to identify the difference between oystercatchers and lapwings or peewits. It was only a mile or so to the shop in the village and I frequently ran errands for Kitten, using the little wicker basket on the handlebars to carry a few messages. On one memorable occasion I hit a bump on the way home and a bag of sugar bounced out onto the road. Although I scooped up as much as I could, I received a severe reprimand for being so careless. It is difficult to believe that sugar rationing, introduced during the war, did not end until 1953.

We relied on Betty-and-her-Mother, and before that her Father, Johnnie, to supply all our basic groceries. And if anything unusual was delivered to their little shop, Betty would ring to let us know. There was huge excitement when the first box of bananas arrived after the war. The family waxed lyrical about these objects which I treated with great suspicion. If you haven't had a banana by the age of two, it's hard to know what all the fuss is about and I was not impressed. Some years later, Betty rang to tell us that a new and unusual fruit had arrived called a vocado. Puddy didn't have the heart to tell her that avocado pears were not only delicious with dressing, but nutritious, and ever after our family referred to them as 'vocados', although not in public of course.

The shop had a counter on three sides with the Post Office section on the left, while various diverse and unrelated objects hung from pegs in the ceiling – gumboots, saucepans, brushes and coal-hods. The shelves behind the counter were neatly stacked with tinned food, jars of macaroni, tubes of toothpaste, and other essentials. Tall square tins were filled with loose biscuits which we ordered by the pound and Johnnie scooped into paper bags to weigh on a handsome set of scales while dispensing a flow of gentle banter. Betty, with her short dark curly hair and bright blue eyes, dealt mainly in gossip. Indeed there was nothing in the surrounding area that Betty-and-her-Mother-or-Father did not know. And if outside the area, they made it their business to find out.

In those days the shop at Fionnphort also served the people of Iona. Although old Mary-Ann ran a small shop beside Iona jetty, the shelves were pitifully empty. If the requested item was not on display, she would disappear and rummage for it in a back room, sometimes with success, more often not. It was hard to work out which of her eyes to follow, for one crossed the other and neither engaged one's own. When asked why she didn't stock shoe-laces, she reportedly replied, 'Och no – if I had shoe-laces everyone would be asking for them!'

Before the war, a cook, two maids and a handyman looked after the family but the war changed everything, just as it did for thousands of households. For a short period after the war we still had one maid, Chrissie, who lived in the cottage, but Kitten was in charge of her own kitchen and all the cooking. This must have been in sharp contrast to her many years in India when, as a memsahib, she became accustomed to the care and attention of numerous household servants from a bearer to a punka-wallah, but she adapted to the change in circumstances and reverted to her traditional island ways with natural ease.

Grandpop's only involvement in domestic affairs came once a week when he rang Willie Campbell, a local farmer, to place an order for meat. Usually a gigot, a leg of mutton, came top of the list. Willie left it in the box inside the gate to save him walking up the drive and we collected the parcel to take to Kitten. She transferred the gigot to a huge black pot filled with water and a variety of vegetables which included carrots, turnips, cabbage, and a handful of barley. This brew bubbled on the stove to create a traditional Scotch Broth which Puddy felt duty-bound to taste at frequent intervals and which would sustain the family for the next few days. The gigot provided the main course of our evening meal. On the first day, Kitten removed it from the pot and, carved like a roast joint, it was deliciously tender and juicy. It was accompanied by dry floury potatoes bursting out of their skins, produced in the sandy soil of Iona. As the week wore on, the meat reappeared in different guises until finally the mincer finished it off to become shepherd's pie.

Sometimes our meat varied from mutton to chicken – or I should say hen, or boiling fowl. Kitten was the keeper of the hens – around thirty of them – and she kept a bucket on a peg at the end of the scullery table into which every vegetable household scrap was scraped. To this she added oatmeal and water to make a dry variant of porridge which the hens loved, and in return they provided us with eggs. But even the most productive hens had off times and stopped producing eggs. They went broody and for this offence they were sentenced to occupy a tea chest suspended from the ceiling upside down with a floor of chicken wire which, over several days, persuaded the luckless bird to resume laying. During the war, eggs had been rationed to one a week and for a period afterwards they were still so precious that they could be posted to deserving friends and relatives in little wooden crates made for the purpose, so we were fortunate indeed. At times, we had such an abundance of eggs that many of them were preserved in large galvanised bins using isinglass, or water glass. These eggs were invaluable for use in baking and Kitten, like many island women, was a supreme baker. Seldom a day went by when she didn't produce a batch of pancakes or scones for tea, cooked on a large iron girdle, their texture like soft clouds and very different from those baked in an oven. As Nicholas observed, her potato scones were sensational – very thin, sloshed with butter, and rolled up, they seldom survived long enough to reach a plate.

Nicholas held a strongly philosophical view of eggs, regarding them, quite rightly, as a miracle, but he could not hide his disdain for hens. He mentioned our handsome multi-coloured cockerel, Geraldo, who strutted his stuff with gentlemanly pride, but he never knew Peggy or Henrietta. Peggy was pure white and lightly built. With the help of Geraldo, she produced a brood of chicks which were her pride and joy, and she displayed all the best qualities of a hen. She enjoyed our company and often wandered into the kitchen just to be with us. When she finally died, Grandpop parcelled her up and sent her to a laboratory for a post-mortem, interested to know what had caused her demise although I don't recall the outcome. Henrietta, a large Rhode Island Red, also had an endearing personality. Because of our regard for her, she never suffered the indignity of being consigned to the tea chest even when she was broody. She lived to die a natural death, and when the time came, she was buried with due ceremony alongside our other household pets.

Hens like Peggy and Henrietta were notable for being different. Inevitably a time came when not even an upturned tea chest could change the average chicken's mind and there was no chance she would lay another egg. The next stop was the pot, but there was a ritual to this. First the hen was caught, and put in the box by the gate to await her fate. Luckily she could never know that Johnnie the Postman would not only deliver the mail to the house, but be her executioner on his way out. He had the ability to dispatch a chicken with the quickest flick of the neck, and return the corpse to the box where Puddy or I would collect it. Next came the feathers, which Kitten plucked deftly, despite the rheumatics which twisted her fingers. She plucked the bird within an empty pillowcase to prevent the feathers drifting all over the kitchen. A few fluffy areas were left which she singed over an open flame before gutting the bird. It was a process which, as a child, I found highly entertaining and the end product, chicken in any form, was always a treat.

The same could also be said for duck, but sadly our ducks seldom survived more than a couple of seasons. Nicholas regarded them with great affection, and there was no doubting they were engaging little characters – running around as a gang, but never doing any damage. They were always destined for the pot, usually to enliven the post-war diet of cousins in the city. On one macabre occasion, four met their maker at the hands of Johnnie-the-Postman and I watched their wings flapping as they hung upside down on a fence. We did not rear ducks just because they were cute.

Rabbit was a different matter. Nicholas was never shy to boast about his prowess at hunting rabbits, but even he had to agree that Puddy was a dab hand with a .410 shotgun and often came home with a brace of rabbits. John was also a good shot, being in the army, but when asked why he preferred to shoot the enemy than rabbits, his reply was simple: 'Because rabbits don't shoot you!' It was Grandpop's job to skin the bunny and I was always an interested spectator, watching as he disembowelled the animal with surgical skill while explaining the function of various parts of anatomy. I was convinced from an early age that I would one day become the first woman surgeon, little realising that this would require other talents besides curiosity.

Sadly, the deliberate introduction to Mull of that repellent disease, myxomatosis, put an end to our appetite for rabbit. It was loathsome to see those ailing creatures, their heads bulging, their eyes weeping as they sat, transfixed, breathing rapidly but barely able to move. Wild rabbit, once freely available, has long been a thing of the past.

Of course there were times when we cursed the rabbits. They persisted in finding every possible route into the vegetable garden, artfully destroying Puddy's attempts at providing Kitten with ingredients for soup. Nevertheless a few bedraggled cabbages and lettuces usually survived. Strawberries occasionally made it to maturity but there were seldom enough to reach the table, while raspberries were by far the most successful fruit, often producing two or three crops every season. By September, the brambles were abundant and Kitten and I would search the hedgerows, filling tin jugs with fruit – red for jam making, black for immediate consumption. There was never any doubt as to who picked what, for my jug was never full.

Kitten made several jars of bramble jam each season and in January she produced enough marmalade – very thick and dark – to last the year. The Seville oranges were delivered to Betty's shop along with the gumboots, saucepans and toothpaste, but one vital product was hard to come by. Bread was delivered only once a week. The loaves, with black and white crusts top and bottom, arrived on Fridays. We would take home a batch of four or five loaves to last the week but as the days passed, blue mould mottled the outside of each loaf until by Thursday the remaining loaf was completely covered by a layer of velvety dust. All surfaces had to be carved off, substantially reducing the size of each slice.

The solution was to make our own bread and it was John, whose love of food had been noted by Nicholas, who turned his talents to bread-making. Mixing the ingredients, covering the bowl with a tea towel, and leaving it to prove by the Aga, before vigorously kneading it, and finally baking it, became part of a daily ritual providing us with a deliciously squidgy loaf which seldom lasted through the day.

Wonderful as the Post Office shop was, there were some items that Betty-and-her-Mother did not stock, and for these, there was no alternative but a trip to Oban.

CHAPTER FIVE

You may think it strange that we needed to travel to the mainland – a journey that took about four hours in each direction by land and sea – when we could have gone to Tobermory on the island. But no buses went to Tobermory from the Ross of Mull, and even if they did, the cost of freight made every item more expensive on the island. So we would leave Achaban early in the morning and set off for Craignure to catch the ferry. The throbbing of the generator to provide electric light always accompanied these early starts in winter, when it was pitch dark.

Sometimes we went by bus; more often we drove Florrie. I should say that Florrie had been confined to the garage throughout the war, for lack of petrol which was only available to those who needed it. She was on wooden blocks to save her tyres, and it was not until well after the war that she was lifted off the blocks and wheeled outside. Willie Gordon, a good friend of the family who, like John, always wore a kilt, came to lunch one day. He knew about cars and, after a very few minutes with his sleeves rolled up, he coaxed life into Florrie's engine.

Puddy took some pride in never having passed a driving test, which did not become compulsory until 1935. She had bought Florrie as a second-hand car for £50 but it was not until after the war that Florrie really earned her keep. I well remember my first excursion on the road with Puddy driving while I clung to the front seat, my nose pressed to the dashboard, convinced she was incapable of coordinating her hands and feet at the same time. I was unable to stifle a squeal of terror when a sheep crossed the road ahead, fearful that Puddy would forget to engage the brake. I need not have worried. She was a very good driver and never had a single accident on Mull or anywhere else.

The drive to Craignure – a distance of around thirty miles – took nearly two hours due to the state of the road. The surface was rough and the route twisty and bumpy. It was single track all the way, with a narrow grass verge and ditch on each side. Tall black and white posts marked passing places along the route, and there was – and still is – a specific but unwritten rule about their use: always stop on the left to allow oncoming vehicles to pass, even if the passing place is on the other side, to avoid any possibility of a collision. And the other is to keep an eye on the mirror, to pull to the side and allow faster traffic to overtake, for it could be a doctor on emergency call. Few things have changed in the past fifty years since the surface of the road was metalled and some sections of the road straightened in the early 1960s.

The first few miles took us through the Ross of Mull with its low-lying hills and a few wizened oak woods. We passed through the neighbouring village of Bunessan, which in those days contained a Post Office, an inn and two churches, but no adequate shops. (It would be many years before the Post Office was transformed into the smallest but best-stocked minimarket imaginable.) The road followed the shoreline of Loch Scridain, a great inlet of sea dividing the Ross from the impressive terraced headland of Burg. In stormy weather, when the wind came from the west, the waterfalls blew upwards, like smoking chimneys. In the distant days of horse travel, Kitten spoke of changing horses at the Kinloch Inn – from Gaelic meaning head of the loch – and this marked the end of the peninsula. At this point, with the shoulder of Mull's only Munro, Ben More, high above, there was a choice of roads. The one to the left led to a spectacular trip to the north end of the island, while on the right, the road to Craignure led through 'The Glen'. It took the best part of an hour to drive along this narrow thread of road through Glen More, with rushes down the centre which swept beneath the car but marked the route when snow fell. There were hazards all the way along: sharp bends, stray sheep, blind summits, narrow hump-back bridges, and dauntless deer with a complete disregard for the highway code, jeopardising both themselves and other road users. Indeed, deer still form the greatest risk to driving in Mull. A heavy fall of snow could close the road, but we would have been warned about this in advance by Betty-or-her-Mother.

Halfway through the Glen the height of the road gave a view overlooking three lochs which so sparked her imagination that Puddy made this the setting for a village, Kilcaraig, which was still in her head but in future years would become the title for her novel, set in Mull and telling the saga of a family with a rather different lifestyle from our own. Without the village of her creation, the Glen was a desolate place, filled with legends of clan battles and the ghosts of headless horse-men. A fourth loch, with a man-made island, home of clan chiefs, was close to an isolated but inhabited cot-tage and the only red telephone box for miles around. Shortly after this, a long bend sent the road in another direction, towards Lochs Spelve and Don. The final run through woodland brought us to the picturesque Craignure Inn and the jetty nearby where we climbed out of the car and looked out for the lopsided *Lochin-var*. When she came in sight, we boarded the tender to be ferried alongside as she heaved and wallowed in the bay. Once safely aboard, we headed for the purser's office to buy our tickets before propping up against the funnel on the upper deck, or descending to the lower deck to chat with fellow passengers while seagulls wheeled and dived in expectation of a bucketful of scraps tossed from the galley.

By the time the *Lochinvar* arrived in Oban we had just over two hours before she sailed again for the return journey. Oban is best seen from the sea and its most distinctive feature is the large tower on the hill resembling Rome's Coliseum, which readily identifies Oban in postcards. McCaig's Tower, known perhaps unjustly as McCaig's Folly in those days, was built at the end of the 1800s to give work to unemployed stone-masons, but Mr McCaig, a philanthropic banker, died before it was completed. Oban did not develop until the railway arrived in 1880, terminating in a pretty Swiss-style station with its appealing clock tower. Every style of architecture was represented along the seafront, and no building matched its neighbour in shape or height. The sleek Marine Hotel was built in the 1930s but its name disappeared when it joined the Scots Baronial Regent Hotel next door. Most of the shops were nearby, in George Street or along the Esplanade. Sometimes we had hospital appointments or visits to make, but more often than not we rushed from shop to shop – McKerchers for groceries and Sawers for fish, which would be delivered to the warehouse on the North Pier.

You may find it strange that we bought fish in Oban when you would think that, living on an island, sur-rounded by sea, we must have plenty of fish swimming all around us. But very few islanders fished commer-cially and the fishing fleet was based at Oban. Kitten sometimes talked about her youth when she fished for saithe in the Sound of Iona – except she called them by the Gaelic *piocach*, using the language which thirty years in India had not expunged. Mackerel, known as 'the scavenger of the sea', was also plentiful but not popular, having a name and reputation which it did not deserve. On the other hand wild salmon was regarded as 'queen of the sea' and for some special occasions, Grandpop placed an order with a local fisherman. It would be a good few years before salmon farming was introduced to Scotland's west coast and this wonderful fish became widely available.

In recent years shellfish have become popular for export, at least until recession started to make an impact. Huge refrigerated trucks collect them every week for processing in Spain and Portugal. Things were very different in the 1950s. Most shellfish had little value and crabs were discarded. Lobsters were the shellfish of choice and I had the child's ghoulish fascination in watching the poor creatures meet their demise in a cauldron of boiling water. My attitude to lobsters changed one day when a sale of work took place in the school. It ended with an auction in which the prize item was a live lobster. I was no more than six or seven and had become detached from Puddy's restraining hand. Standing at the front of the crowd for a clear view of the proceedings, I started to communicate with the auctioneer using a series of gestures which he interpreted as affirmative. To Puddy's horror, ownership of the lobster finally transferred to me for an exorbitant price which, of course, she had to pay. My penalty was to share the back seat of Florrie with the large crustacean, albeit contained within a shallow box lid. Brandishing its giant claws and waving its antennae, it paced around in a distinctly menacing manner. Although I later adopted a taste for prawns, I have never cared much for lobster and I have always been wary of auctions.

Clothing was not available on the island so Puddy or Kitten placed orders with Jenners in Edinburgh, but more often than not we found what we needed in Oban. Chalmers Highland Tweed Warehouse sold tweed skirts and twinsets, while the large gallery at the rear was filled with bales of cloth to buy by the yard and be made to measure. Although it stocked a range of tartan, the one we preferred was Kitten's which had to be specially ordered. Of course, I had little say in buying clothes. Like most little girls of the time, I usually wore a kilt or plain pleated skirt with a Fair Isle jumper which other little girls of my generation will immediately remember as being agonisingly scratchy and uncomfortable, but complaints and grimacing faces were ignored and there was nothing for it but to put up with it.

Growing fast, I often needed new shoes and Huttons was just along the road from Chalmers. It was a dark but lofty store, lined to the roof with shelves stacked high with shoe boxes. Before the dangers of radiation were recognised, it was fun to try on shoes, put your feet into an X-ray machine, and peer through the window at the top to watch your toes waggling within the outline of nails which defined the shape of the shoe. Satisfied that they fitted correctly, they joined the other packages we collected during our shopping trip.

If we had time, we stopped at Kennedy's tearoom where the restaurant upstairs served scones and biscuits on triple-layered cake stands, and the waitresses, dressed in black with crisp white aprons and caps, wrote our order on little pads attached to their waist by string. Before we left, they counted how many cakes we had eaten, and charged us accordingly. Downstairs a selection of cakes, pies and pastries could be bought from the counter. These too would be added to our packages as we rejoined the *Lochinvar* for the long journey home.

Few visits to Oban passed without the need for pills, potions, or toiletries of some sort which could only be found at Boots the chemist, which occupied an imposing corner site on George Street. Our local doctor was a good friend of the family, but we seldom called upon him because Grandpop, being a doctor, could prescribe medicines and he sometimes placed orders by telephone with Boots, which he then received by post. Otherwise bicarbonate of soda was his remedy of choice for almost all family complaints, and very efficient it was too. When Puddy wasn't draped over the Aga, sipping soup, she was clutching a mug of hot water and soda-bicarb to calm her indigestion, and a paste of soda-bicarb provided an excellent poultice for insect bites and other skin conditions.

We usually managed to complete our shopping before the boat left at 1.15, but occasionally we needed more time ashore, to visit patients in the little Cottage Hospital, or attend the out-patient clinic. We then took advantage of the change of schedule each Wednesday when the boat called at Lismore and remained in Oban until three o'clock. This enabled island farmers to attend livestock auctions at the mart, when Oban took on quite a lively appearance as sheep and cattle were herded through the town accompanied by keen-eyed border collies and shepherds, each with a crook or cromack in hand, a flat hat, and a raincoat slung over the shoulder. I never landed on Lismore but, unlike Craignure, the boat tied alongside and this weekly sailing gave the impression to those of us who watched passengers going up and down the gangplank that it was almost off the map.

The greatest annual event in Oban was the Argyllshire Gathering, known as the Oban Games, which in those days coincided with the start of the new school term towards the end of September. Each year I had no option but to spend all day in Oban waiting for the sleeper train in the evening and I always sought refuge in the Station Hotel. The Highland Games took place the day before, followed by a ball which would not end till the wee small hours. So I sat in a corner of the lounge and watched a succession of bleary-eyed men and women, looking somewhat the worse for wear, emerging into the bright light of day. They exchanged greetings with one another, their strident voices filling the room. The clan system may have died a death many years before, but rivalry lived on, for it was a well-accepted fact that Macleans and their adherents stayed at the Station Hotel, while Campbells and the House of Argyll maintained a presence at the elegant Great Western, on the Esplanade.

But to return to shopping trips: every so often, we needed an item which could not be found in Mull or Oban. An order would be placed by post and the goods shipped from Glasgow. The old steamship *Dunara Castle* was a general cargo boat which supplied the islands, sailing from Glasgow once a week. She had been doing so since she was launched on the Clyde in 1875, and had a place in history, having enabled the evacuation of St Kilda in 1930 by carrying livestock and surplus goods to the mainland. Tormore obscured a view of the sea from behind Achaban, but a plume of black smoke indicated the approach of the old ship behind the hill. I stood at the back gate, looking out for the tell-tale sign, eager to alert the family. Archie-the-Carrier would pick up the goods from the jetty, for delivery to the house. This was an early memory for it was not long before this convenient arrangement came to an end. After seventy years of faithful service, the *Dunara Castle* was scrapped in the river of her birth.

Other items, such as coal, were delivered by the ubiquitous 'puffers', the little steamboats that were a famous sight throughout the west coast. Their tubby design allowed them to be beached and unloaded without the need for a pier or jetty and they could set off again on the next rising tide. The puffers also delivered the fuel we needed for heating, lighting and driving. Huge drums of petrol and paraffin were brought by Archie-the-Carrier and stored in the old corrugated-iron shed, which had been occupied by the hens before they moved to the smart new henhouse built by Grandpop and John.

Almost all our needs were met one way or the other, but there was one product which neither love nor money could easily supply: fresh milk. An enduring solution to this problem brought about a very pleasant addition to our lives.

CHAPTER SIX

Milk was hard to come by in a land where cattle were bred for meat. Each year, cows produced enough milk to feed their calves and no more. There were few dairy farmers on Mull and none close to us. Most of the locals used condensed milk in their tea and coffee, which produced a peculiar aroma before taste confirmed that it came out of a tin. Instead of using condensed milk, we relied upon our closest neighbour, old John Maclean, to provide us with milk. He kept a dairy cow and lived across the Dalvan, a stretch of moorland which separated his croft from the grounds of Achaban. Old and lame though he was, he came across the bog every day, supporting himself on a stick with one hand and carrying a can of milk in the other. He arrived just in time for elevenses and sat on a chair in the kitchen, bringing us up to date with local gossip, before heading back across the Dalvan with an empty can. Never shy about speaking his mind, on one memorable occasion he hailed Margie's arrival home for her summer holiday with the words: 'My, Miss Nelson, you're fine and stout!' This was by way of a compliment which, needless to say, she took very much to heart.

His milk, though small in quantity, was beautifully rich and produced a thick layer of cream when left in a bowl for a while. Kitten sometimes put a good dollop or two in an old syrup tin with the lid firmly closed and, sitting in the kitchen, she shook the tin up and down vigorously, while the liquid slurped rhythmically. After about twenty minutes the slurping transformed to knocking and, upon removing the lid, a beautiful lump of butter dropped out which she batted into shape with a pair of wooden hands. The days when butter was produced in a tall, cylindrical wooden butter churn, using a pumping action, were already long gone.

This arrangement was satisfactory so long as old John Maclean's cow continued to produce milk, but just as hens stop laying eggs, cows stop yielding milk. In this case the upside-down tea chest was not an option. Puddy decided it was time to do something about the situation. She bought a book about goat husbandry, and she asked John and Grandpop to build a lean-to shed, suitable for goats, at the end of the barn. There was only one thing for it, and that was to buy a goat.

Puddy had one other problem to overcome, which was not so easily covered by reading books and does not come naturally to those who have never done it. She needed to learn the technique of milking. Here again, old John Maclean came to the rescue. He invited

Puddy and me to try our hand at milking his cow. Now it is quite obvious that a cow with four teats is different from a goat with two. But that is not the only difference. Goats are smaller and lower and they move faster, all of which Puddy was to learn in due course. Old John Maclean's cow was in the byre beside his cottage and we entered through the low doorway with some trepidation. Adjusting our eyes to the darkness, we saw for the first time exactly where our milk came from and it was not entirely reassuring. The soil on the floor was soft and spongy and our feet sank an inch or two. Old John Maclean eased himself onto an upturned bucket, used as a stool, and selected a fresh bucket which he put under the cow. He then demonstrated the art of milking before offering the bucket-stool to Puddy. She had been practising the five-finger exercise motion under the pew in church for the past few weeks – squeezing the thumb and forefinger first and then the others in a ripple effect. This time it was for real, and her first few attempts made little progress while the cow stamped irritably. Then she found her rhythm and we both marvelled at the satisfying sound of milk jetting into the bucket, forming froth on the surface. The bucket was soon filled and Puddy stood up, having completed her session. But the cow still had more milk to give so, unperturbed, old John Maclean set aside the fresh bucket and lifted the one which had been used as a stool. Putting it upright, he proceeded to direct the remaining milk into it. Puddy and I glanced at each other, thankful that we would know in future exactly where our milk supply came from.

The next problem was to find a goat breeder. This was long before it became fashionable to keep goats, so breeders were few and far away. However, one farmer in the north of Mull bred British Saanens and Puddy made an arrangement to buy one from him. I was with her when we took the back seat out of Florrie and started off in the direction of Kinloch but this time we avoided Glen More by taking the left fork in the road. It was a spectacular drive, round the base of Ben More, traversing Glen Seilisdeir – the glen of irises – to dramatic views of the sea on the left, and the ship-like shape of Staffa with the Treshnish Isles in the distance. The road clung to a narrow ledge between the dark waters of Loch-na-Keal and the Gribun Rocks towering above, threatening to crumble at any moment. Indeed, we passed a huge boulder where legend held that a newly married couple were crushed to death in the little cottage beneath, a story which did not fail to appeal to me. Shortly beyond this a sheep fank, with a dry-stone wall, provided a convenient stopping point in more ways than one, for trees are few and far between on Mull, and rocks provide little protection from bird watchers with their binoculars. We then continued to the far side of the loch, until we reached the farm in a beautiful spot overlooking the Isle of Ulva.

After meeting Arnish, and admiring her smooth white coat and neat little beard, we coaxed her into the back of the car with a huge bunch of kale before setting off on the long drive home. Our passenger was perfectly content and arrived at Achaban none the worse for her journey. Puddy, hard up though she was, never stinted on things of importance and Arnish was no exception. She had won first prize for milking at the Royal Highland Show and had the udders to prove it. There was no going back now. She needed to be milked, and Puddy was the only one with any know-how. And so, after introducing Arnish to her new accommodation – a single stall, with a manger full of fresh kale – Puddy sat on her new three-legged milking stool and proceeded to practise what she had learnt. Arnish chewed the cud patiently. She had the wisdom of maturity to tolerate Puddy's inept handling but it was not long before Puddy got the hang of Arnish's two teats, in a manner of speaking, and filled the bucket to a satisfactory level.

Even I, a faddy child, soon became accustomed to the taste of goat's milk which, with a little sugar added, tasted no different from cow's milk. In addition to butter, Kitten sometimes boiled the milk, collecting the curds in a muslin cloth and hanging it up to drip until soft cheese formed.

The relationship between Puddy and Arnish blossomed and Puddy soon decided to invest in a companion for Arnish. Flora was also a British Saanen but not so heavily built as Arnish. They both had bright yellow eyes and trim beards, and their knees clicked as they walked, so we could always hear them coming. And that was another difference between cows and goats: cows need to be herded whereas our goats came to the call. This was demonstrated when Puddy went away on one of her occasional holidays, leaving Margie in charge. Margie had never learnt to milk and was averse to trying, so she asked Wee Sandy from the village to help her. He was accustomed to cows and started to jump up and down and wave his arms to drive the goats into their shed, whereupon they turned tail and, clicking their knees, set off in the opposite direction. He soon discovered that all he had to do was call them and they would willingly come.

Wee Sandy was one of several men in the district who had been rescued from the festering slums of 1930s Glasgow and boarded out to foster homes in the islands. Questions were sometimes raised about the scheme, which supplied workers on the crofts in return for board and lodging, but there was no doubting that Wee Sandy was always willing to give a helping hand wherever it was needed and appeared to benefit from the outdoor life.

Arnish and Flora became good friends and certainly had a way of communicating with each other. Nicholas clearly had a better understanding of what they had to say than we did. But even we noticed that they could spend several days munching away at a whin bush only to make a spontaneous and combined decision to discard it in favour of a pile of old copies of the *British Medical Journal* ready for a bonfire.

Our domestic life changed little from day to day. Puddy was always up first to feed and milk the goats. Grandpop made a pot of tea, using a tin kettle on a Primus stove, which he and Kitten shared in their bedroom. He used the Indian term *chota hazri* for this early morning ritual. Later on, the sound of scraping toast indicated that breakfast was ready. We started with porridge, which Kitten prepared the night before to steep beside the Aga. Although solid, it was smooth textured and floated when milk was added, rotating in the bowl as we took each spoonful. I added sugar; Grandpop preferred salt. In winter it was dark until nearly ten in the morning when we set about our daily chores.

When she was at home, which wasn't often, Margie did the housework, but usually Kitten attacked the piles of washing. She used a washboard to scrub sheets and left them to soak in the deepest of the two sinks in the scullery before threading them through the mangle. I sometimes helped by turning the handle. If the weather was dry, she stretched the sheets out on the grass to bleach, taking care that Arnish and Flora were not anywhere near in case they developed a taste for linen.

Puddy and John spent the morning out of doors. Although Arnish and Flora had plenty of space to roam around the back of the house, with a wild field all to themselves, they frequently tested the boundaries and soon spotted any weakness in the fencing. It was always easier for Puddy when John was home on leave

My great-grandfather bought the Free Kirk Manse, which once served the kirk two miles up the road and not St Ernan's Church by the loch.

In the mid 1930s the old manse, renamed Achaban House, was modernised and extended, and the beautiful Tormore granite covered by roughcast.

Within a month of my birth in London, my mother, Puddy, brought me to Achaban to escape the Blitz. Here we are sitting on the bench outside the dining-room window.

I had only recently met my grandparents for the first time when this photo of Kitten and me was taken. The standing stone, east of Achaban, is in the background.

When our water supply failed, I went with John and Kitten to fill buckets from the well. We were not so jaunty when the buckets were full!

John built a little jetty into the loch while I provided him with pebbles and other building material.

John built me a model yacht, and I enjoyed sailing it on the end of a fishing line under the guidance of Grandpop.

I spent a lot of time on my own in or around the loch, just splashing about or sailing the model yacht. St Ernan's Church is in the background.

My bicycle gave me the freedom of the road, but I spent many hours just pedalling around the house, making up stories as I went.

Our black Labrador, Bruce, became a close companion, but he stayed with us for less than three years due to his split personality. Florrie the Ford is in the background.

I always felt my help was valued – even when pulling an empty wheelbarrow!

Nicholas the Cat sunning himself beside Kitten on the bench outside the dining-room.

Corrieshellach could carry heavy loads in her panniers. Here she is with John and Grandpop outside the old henhouse, wearing her thick winter coat.

The weather was good on the day of the Bunessan Show so Grandpop and I dressed smartly, but we did not show Carla.

Above. After Corrie won her class at the Royal Highland Show, Puddy wanted to show her off at the Bunessan Show although there was no pony class. Puddy rode the five miles to Bunessan and back.

Right. Margie and Lottie were inseparable. Lottie was followed by Sophie and then Cora, each black poodle smaller than the last.

Puddy gave Corrieshellach's filly foal to Mr Cairns, her Perth breeder, in return for preparing Corrie for the Royal Highland Show. He named the foal Annabel, and was rewarded when she became Champion Highland Pony in 1959.

Grandpop admired his handiwork after making a milking frame for Flora, watched by the kids.

I spent many hours in my little flat-bottomed dinghy, exploring the loch and its islands.

Puddy, me, Margie with Lottie and my school friend Di talk to a friend at the Salen Show, 1956.

The weather on 13 August 1956 was atrocious, so we were amazed to see HM The Queen arrive at Craignure, having been let down the side of *Britannia* in a barge.

Puddy, looking windswept, on the jetty at Craignure watches the Queen as a police officer ushers her into the passenger seat of the car.

Above. The view of
Loch Poit-na-I (Pottie)
changed constantly but
never failed to please.
This photo was taken
from upstairs at
Achaban.

Right. Carla's aunt was
Tracey Witch of Ware,
twice Supreme
Champion of Crufts,
yet Carla's beauty failed
to impress the judge of
the Fancy Dogs at the
Salen Show!

to help her driving in the stobs and straining the wire but, despite her small size – and she was only five foot two – she was strong and well able to restore a dry-stone wall on her own if necessary. It was as important to keep sheep out as it was to keep our goats in.

In due course, when their milk supply began to decline, the goats were introduced to a billy goat who lived nearby and their subsequent kids duly arrived, two each, including a billy for Arnish. Fortunately for Arnish, Willie Campbell did not use his humane killer on the billy but gave him to his little daughter to keep as a pet. Flora's little nanny, called Mairi, joined her mother and Arnish in the goat shed and between them they continued to provide us with all the milk we needed.

When he wasn't building goat sheds or hen houses, Grandpop hummed his hums, puffed on his pipe, and disappeared into Alistair's room where he turned his hand to bodging. I should explain that I never knew Alistair. Long before the war, he worked as butler-cum-handyman-cum-chauffeur for the family and he lived in this little room between the barn and the garage. Apart from a small black stove which had become rusted with age, it had no comforts and he shared an outside lava-tory with the maids from the cottage. Over the years since he left, the room had become a workshop. It was intensely gloomy but a small square window permit-ted a narrow shaft of daylight to illuminate the work bench.

Living on an island required two essential qualities: resourcefulness and improvisation, and Grandpop was master of both. Besides all the usual hand tools, he kept little tin boxes harbouring an assortment of small objects which were never thrown out in case they might prove useful: curtain rings, bottle tops, you name it. With no local handymen, or hardware store nearby, Grandpop could be relied upon to repair and maintain most household objects. And if he could find no other solution he turned to old Meccano pieces which, in his hands, had the uncanny ability to make do or mend just about anything. Grandpop called this bodging, but he was unduly severe on himself. He took infinite care, fashioning washers out of old hot-water bottles, or splicing broken rods with fishing line.

'It's all do-it-yourself here!' said Kitten, coining the phrase long before it became common currency.

It was just as well Grandpop was so handy. His skills were often put to the test by the various mechanical implements that were intended to make life easier for us, and the electric generator was a case in point. As well as lighting, we relied upon it for our water supply.

CHAPTER SEVEN

Achaban was originally built as a manse in the mid 1800s. As Nicholas rightly recorded, it was not the manse of the little church nearby, but of another a mile or so away. This was due to the many splits in the Church of Scotland after the Reformation, resulting in a number of different congregations forming, all of which required their own church building.

The granite house stood in an exposed position on the moor overlooking pretty Loch Poit-na-hi – the pot of Iona – but always called Pottie with the emphasis on the second syllable. The walls were three feet thick and small windows helped protect it from gales blowing in from the Atlantic. Kitten's father bought the house after the churches once more combined and there was no requirement for a separate manse. It was a modest house with a drawing-room and dining-room at the front, divided by a hall which led to a small morning-room and kitchen at the back. Its spacious landing gave access to five bedrooms upstairs, four of which had fireplaces, but there the comforts ended.

In the mid 1930s Kitten and Grandpop set about an

ambitious scheme of improvements. While they and the family took refuge in another house a few miles away, a team of builders, painters and decorators set about modernising Achaban. They ripped out the old Victorian cast-iron fireplaces and buried them in the bog at the back of the house where they would resurface many years later. They added a study-cum-library to the dining-room, with views to the south and east, and they enlarged and altered the windows at the front, making fashionable bay windows to the drawing-room and bedroom above. This alteration was to become an endless source of annoyance and perplexity as rain accompanied by a south-west wind consistently found its way to the window where it dripped from the frame. Despite all attempts to discover its source, even by Grandpop, there was nothing for it but to pull the furniture away from the window and arrange buckets to catch the drips.

While unwanted water provided a challenge, the need for 'all mod cons' had become essential in a modern house. In addition to running water in the kitchen, a bathroom was built on to the back of the house, and basins installed in each bedroom.

Crenellations, like a castle, adorned the flat roofs of the additional rooms, the study and the porch, a pretentious addition that was not entirely appreciated by the family, while the pretty pink granite walls were hidden by a protective covering of roughcast that turned a depressing shade of battleship-grey when it rained.

The kitchen, with its black range (the Aga would come later) and large press, providing space for all the household china, were left unaltered, but a scullery was added with a window looking east and a pair of ceramic sinks, one shallow and one deep, provided plenty of room for washing both dishes and clothes.

The most ambitious innovation, however, was the introduction of electricity. Home-cured bacon was forsaken for the wonders of electric light when a generator was installed in the pig shed. Sparked by an assortment of batteries and accumulators, the engine ran on petrol which was not expensive at the time. Any switch in the house could set it off – in theory. In practice it needed frequent coaxing and cajoling but, once running, it cost the same no matter how many lights were on – in fact, the more, and the brighter, the merrier. In winter it became the tradition to welcome visitors or members of the family by switching all the lights on. Their bright twinkle must have been a novel sight in an area where the soft glow of oil lamps was barely visible at a distance, and street lighting unknown.

Not all our visitors understood the vagaries of our lighting system. They sometimes walked into their rooms and flicked the light switch inadvertently. It was a natural thing to do. After a shudder and a splutter, the engine started throbbing and soon the whole household was alert. At other times, no amount of trying would turn the lights on, and then Grandpop retired to the engine house with his little boxes of oddments, an oil can, and a small hammer in the hope that one or other or all three would have the desired result.

Although it lit the house efficiently, the electric lighting plant had its limitations. There were no power points. Instead of Alternating Current, the generator used Direct Current for which there were few electric appliances other than an iron with a flex which sprang from the light socket in the ceiling, and a snake-like vacuum cleaner. Neither of these were very efficient and the iron was positively hazardous. Kitten continued to press the laundry by heating a couple of black irons on top of the range, swapping them over as each cooled down, while Margie preferred a simple carpet sweeper to remove the dirt, most of which was underfoot.

In addition, the engine caused severe interference on the radio, which was totally self-defeating. John's regiment was once stationed in Berlin, and he brought home a Grundig radio which looked very smart and occupied a prime position in the drawing room, but it was rendered useless by the generator which operated it. As both could not run at the same time, we had to switch off the lights and listen to the Roberts wireless in the kitchen. Although ostensibly portable, it contained a large battery which made it too heavy to carry easily from room to room.

This situation controlled our night-time routine. Before the advent of universal television – which of course we did not have – every household in the land tuned into the nine o'clock news. It was the high point of every evening and for us prompted a somewhat singular ritual when we turned off the generator so that we could listen to the news by the light of oil lamps.

There was a table in the lobby outside the kitchen where the lamps were assembled every morning. Kitten topped them up with paraffin, trimmed the wicks, and cleaned the glass chimneys with twists of newspaper. As soon as darkness fell, or just before nine o'clock if the engine had been on, Puddy or Grandpop lit the lamps. Each wick was kept low until the glass chimney had time to heat – raise too quickly and it might burst. If the wicks were turned too high, thick smoke blackened the glass, and if the paraffin burned too low, the wicks glowed a fiery red and emitted an unpleasantly pungent smell.

Small single-wick lamps were stationed at strategic places around the house – in the hall, on the landing, in the kitchen, the scullery, the cloakroom – where they would glow all evening. A couple of tall double-wick lamps spread a gracious glow over the drawing room, but they were supplemented in time by two Tilley lamps which provided strong light wherever we assembled. They were pressure lamps and their mantles were lit by a special procedure. A small reservoir of felt soaked in methylated spirits was clipped round the neck of each lamp and set alight, allowing the flame to heat the mantle. Vigorous pumping raised the pressure in the lamp until, at the optimum moment, a small knob was turned and the mantle blazed into a fierce bright light. This moment was not always predictable. Sometimes tall flames flared high and licked the low ceiling. This scared me as a child and I kept a respectful distance at all times when the lamps were being lit.

Puddy also used a Tilley storm lantern which could be taken out of doors. This was excellent for lighting the outhouses and she used it in the goat house when she was milking, but Grandpop never took it into Alistair's room, preferring to rely on touch and feel. On other occasions we used torches to check the hens, or the cattle in The Fence. This large field was unusual as it was surrounded by wire fencing, rather than a dry-stone wall, hence its name. All around was moorland, so the field must once have been drained and cultivated. Kitten thought that potatoes once grew there, but it was hard to believe. Puddy decided it would make a good home for a few cattle, so she invested in a registered herd, Tom, Dick and Harry, and was overjoyed when she sold them at the end of the season, bringing home banknotes, the size of which she had never seen before. She did not mind seeing Tom, Dick and Harry leave on the cattle boat at Bunessan to spend the winter on rich pastures in the south and, encouraged by her success, she invested in two more bullocks, Peter and Iain, and a little Highland heifer. But this time, her luck ran out. She bought the heifer at a local sale but there was a delay in its delivery. Although this was a blow at the time, it was just as well. The dreadful epidemic of foot and mouth disease was identified, and all animals bought at that sale were slaughtered. If the heifer had been delivered, our goats and cattle would have ended in the lime pits along with all the other cloven-hoofed animals in the district. Puddy was distressed by the loss of the cow, and by the whole foot and mouth episode. But her greatest sorrow was the loss of Iain who did not survive the season. Puddy sometimes let Peter and Iain join the local cattle on the moorland around us, which was common grazing, but Iain fell in a bog and was drowned. Farming was never going to be easy, but that year of 1952 was more challenging than most.

In summer it was light enough to check the cattle until late into the night without any need for torches, but darkness came early in the winter when we drew the curtains before four o'clock in the afternoon. The silent march of the shadows across the walls as we carried the lamps from room to room, the soporific hiss of the Tilleys as their light imperceptibly dimmed during the course of the evening, and the warm smell of paraffin evoked the comforts of home. A brisk pumping action soon restored their brilliance and we could listen to the nine o'clock news without interference.

'It's just the same as the one o'clock news,' Grandpop would grumble, disappointed that no earth-shattering event had occurred since lunchtime.

There was one news story which no amount of television could have made any more vivid to the imagination. The plight of the *Flying Enterprise* will be remembered by all those who listened to the frequent bulletins while the drama unfolded. On her way from Hamburg with a mixed cargo and several passengers on board, *Flying Enterprise* met a storm in the English Channel on Christmas Day, 1951. During the next few days her cargo shifted irretrievably, and she issued an SOS on 28th December. Two ships responded and evacuated her passengers but her Captain, Kurt Carlsen, refused to leave his ship. By 3rd January 1952, the tug *Turmoil* had arrived on the scene, and her mate, Kenneth Dancy, joined Captain Carlsen on *Flying Enterprise* and a tow line was set up with the help of other tugs. We intently followed the entire progress of the courageous little tug *Turmoil* as she attempted to tow *Flying Enterprise* to Falmouth. We were dismayed when the tow line broke, delighted when other tugs joined the rescue, and relieved when Captain Carlsen and Kenneth Dancy finally agreed to abandon ship, seeking refuge aboard *Turmoil* less than an hour before *Flying Enterprise* sank to the bottom of the sea, to a salute of whistles, sirens and foghorns, on 6th January. For more than a week it was all we talked about, and I was moved to create a series of pencil drawings based on the pictures conjured up by the radio.

Although this happened far away, the distant moan of the sea even on a calm day never ceased to remind us of its presence and we knew too many young men who had fallen foul of its uneven temper. One of them, George Clyne, manned the ferry boats between Craignure jetty and the *Lochinvar* twice daily, even in treacherous weather. He never failed to offer a helping hand with a cheerful smile. One evening a storm blew up and, concerned about his boats anchored in the bay, he set out alone to check them. He was never seen alive again. The sea could be cruel indeed.

There was one other event which occurred that Christmas Day in 1951. Like many little girls before me, I was horse mad although I was never a confident rider. I seldom ventured beyond a jog-trot and if, perchance, the horse broke into a canter, I had a tendency to do an involuntary slow-motion dismount. Despite my lack of talent, I cherished ambitions to become a great showjumper and, whenever possible, I went with Puddy to horse shows and gymkhanas, strictly as a spectator of course.

Christmas Day started much like any other, gathering together in Kitten and Grandpop's bedroom where he had prepared tea for us all. We opened our pillowcases in a rota, eldest first, so I always had to wait patiently until my turn came, but this meant we never missed seeing each other's presents opened. Finally all the pillowcases were empty except mine, which had a stray card at the bottom. I checked Puddy's handwriting on the envelope and, opening it quickly, found a photograph of a pony inside. It was a very beautiful pony, but that is all it was: a photograph. Then Puddy said, 'We are going to meet Corrieshellach next week, on your way back to school.' And so our lovely Corrie entered our lives, and in due course became Nicky's closest friend.

CHAPTER EIGHT

Highland ponies are the largest of the native breeds in Britain. They are famed for their even temper and sure-footedness over rough and boggy terrain. Corrieshellach had those qualities and many more. When Puddy and I met her for the first time at a farm near Perth, it was quite obvious that the photograph, in black and white, did not do her justice. She was a great beauty. Described by her breeder as silver dun, she was the colour of fine oatmeal, with a black eel stripe down her spine, typical of Highlanders. She was quite rotund, so not an ideal riding pony, and we were given the choice of another pony of more slender build, but Corrie had already won our hearts.

It was possible at the time to buy a good quality pony for around fifty pounds but Corrie cost twice as much. Living on a war widow's pension did not give Puddy much scope to become a spendthrift but, as I said before, she never stinted on the things that really mattered and to her it really mattered that Corrie should pull her weight – quite literally. Corrie had spent much of her life among the hills of Perthshire, carrying deer during the stalking season, but she had also been schooled for driving. She had the strength to do a range of work which would help Puddy over the years to come, and it was not long after her arrival at Acha-ban that she was put to good use. Puddy located and ordered a dog-cart to be delivered from the mainland.

I well remember the first time we attempted to attach Corrie to the trap. None of us had ever harnessed a horse before so Puddy found an instruction manual, with diagrams explaining which bit of leather did what. At first it was hard to work out the relationship between the illustrations in the manual and the tangle of leather which, even when spread out on the ground, looked very complicated. Crupper – martingale – traces – each had to be put on in a certain order. Enlisting Corrie's co-operation was no problem. Throughout her ordeal, she stood patiently, while we tried first this, then that, and I have no doubt there were a few arguments which she ignored with no more than a flick of her long tail and a twitch of her ears. It was only when we slipped Corrie between the shafts of the trap that the purpose of each part of the harness became clear for the first time. Handling reins for driving was a different skill from riding, but, with a little practice, we soon learnt the art and, to tell the truth, Corrie did not have much option but to travel the road ahead. With so few cars on the road, at speeds no more than twenty miles an hour, they seldom posed a problem, and neither did Corrie.

Corrie took everything in her stride, including the weather. Each winter, an extra layer of soft hair reinforced her coat against the worst of the cold, wind and rain. She appeared fatter than ever, but it made her impervious to the Force 10 gales and driving rain which beat across the Atlantic, with the low-lying Isle of Iona our only shield. It could be a battering, buffeting wind and, apart from a row of stunted trees, slanting towards the east, there was no shelter in the little field below the house where Corrie spent most of her time. We always knew which way the wind was blowing because she would set herself firmly four-square against the worst of the gales. Being fastidious, she turned briefly only to allow for the call of nature.

Corrie remained outside all year round but on really stormy nights, we brought her to the back of the house, away from the prevailing south-west winds. Achaban's exposed position on high ground gave little protection, but it was comforting for us to know she could find a sheltered spot by the back door. It is difficult to imagine the strength of a wind that could make a granite house shudder, that a single gust could tear the ridging off the barn, overturn the duck house, or as Nicholas put it so colourfully, whip the milking stool from its place by the goat house and carry it through the sky like a kite.

We always listened to the shipping forecast, which gave better warning than the usual weather forecast. As John said, the weather was usually past us by the time we heard about it. So each evening we tuned into the radio in the kitchen and waited for those evocative names: Rockall, Malin, Hebrides – Malin being the headland off Northern Ireland that gave its name to our shipping area – but the three were usually combined, sharing the seas to the west of Scotland. If a gale Force 9 or over was predicted, we took special precautions to batten down the hatches, ensuring all the outhouse doors were firmly secured, and that any moveable object was tied down, anchored by boulders if necessary.

A gale could blow relentlessly for several days. On one such occasion the second day fell on a Sunday. It was our habit to attend the little church nearby where the service was held at three o'clock in the afternoon, not a time to claim our full attention, but the Minister came over from Iona, after conducting the service in the little parish church there in the morning, so we felt duty-bound to join his small congregation each Sunday. Usually Kitten and Grandpop, Puddy, John and Margie walked the short distance to church while I pedalled my bicycle, ringing my bell and scattering all and sundry as I went by. On this occasion Margie was not at home and Puddy and John agreed to represent the family, leaving the very old and young behind because the storm was at its height, and it was almost impossible to walk upright. I watched from the upstairs window as they were swept to church by a following wind. They found the minister on his own and, as all three had made the effort to turn up, he elected to go ahead with his prepared service, including a lengthy sermon. Just as he reached his final point, a loud bang brought his oration to an abrupt end as the narrow window behind the pulpit burst into a hundred fragments. History never recorded the theme of his sermon, but there was plenty to report about their struggle home, sometimes taking to the ditch to avoid being blown over.

The Ross of Mull, being low lying and far to the west, has almost the lowest rainfall in the British Isles, whereas the interior of Mull has a lot of rain due to the cluster of mountains in the centre, which attracts the formation of clouds. On one occasion I joined a small group for a walk to the top of Ben More, Mull's highest mountain at 3,169 ft (966m). It was a magnificent balmy day in June, with a clear blue sky. Having scrambled over the scree to reach the summit we were rewarded with an astonishing view of the islands of the west spread out before us. But my most prevailing memory is that of the little clusters of vapour which gathered out of the clear blue sky. Coming together, with apparent magnetic attraction, they formed a cloud and passed overhead, drifting gently to the east to join all the other clouds covering the mainland like a billowy eiderdown.

The weather could be localised: it might be pouring with rain in Bunessan and dry as a bone in Ardtun less than two miles away. The view from the scullery window looked east towards Ben Lee, a low hill behind

Bunessan, which acted as a barometer. If we couldn't
see Lee it must be raining, just as stripes on the loch
were a portent of wilder weather to come.

Although it snowed in the depth of winter, it very
seldom lay around us, but the Glen road was sometimes
blocked for a day or two. One winter we had severe bliz-
zards, resulting in deep snow drifts in the garden which
gave lots of scope for fun: collapsing into the soft snow,
sliding down the slope, and building a snowman with
anthracite eyes. The Glen road was blocked and for the
first and only time I was unable to return to school.
But my joy at gaining three extra days' holiday was
countered by the work I had to do to make up for lost
time in the classroom. This was an exception, just as it
was rare to endure severe frost and even more unusual
for the loch to freeze over. Kitten could remember this
happening frequently in her youth, when the young
lads of the neighbourhood skated to the islands, but
thick ice seldom formed while I was a child.

Kitten and Grandpop had become accustomed to
the heat of India, so along with all the other altera-
tions to the house, they added a conservatory. Built
on the west side of Achaban, the sun parlour formed
a suntrap from midday and it could become intensely
hot. Like many Scots, Kitten did not believe in killing
spiders – something to do with Robert the Bruce –
with the result that webs festooned the panes of glass,
each occupied by a hefty spider. I took morbid delight
in watching unsuspecting flies zoom into the net, to be

caught and wrapped up like a parcel. It never occurred to me at the time that this sanctuary for spiders might have seemed a trifle eccentric to some of our visitors. So far as I am aware, none of them ran away screaming.

It was quite normal for friends to drop in unexpectedly but we could usually see them coming up the drive in time to put the kettle on the stove. Kitten ensured there was always plenty to eat and no-one was allowed to leave the house without being offered food or drink appropriate to the time of day. Tea or coffee and biscuits were produced in the morning for elevenses. If guests were invited for afternoon tea, Kitten spread a pretty lace cloth on a folding side table and dispensed dainty sandwiches in the drawing room. More often, we sat round the dining table, its white cloth covered with plates of scones and pancakes so that everyone could help themselves to butter balls, jam and honey before starting on the cakes. Dinner parties were rare – distances were too great – but if friends came for lunch, we expected them to stay for tea, a reward for travelling such a long way.

Ministers were the exception. They came from Iona to preach at our Sunday afternoon service, and had to forgo tea to catch the ferry back. One young minister was new to the parish and nervousness compelled him to talk without stopping throughout the main course. This was followed by a large jam tart which Puddy brought straight from the Aga. Typically, there was no steam to indicate its heat. The minister was still haranguing us when he took a large bite. Suddenly his cheeks went puce, his eyes popped, and his mouth dropped open as he gasped for air. No-one had thought to warn the poor man that, cool though it looked, the jam was scorching hot. From then on, jam tart was known by the family as Minister's Pudding.

When we didn't have guests, we often had high tea in the kitchen, a meal which included everything imaginable, and was early in the evening, or we had Scotch broth followed by grey stew, but every so often we had a special occasion. 'We'll have a *burra khana*,' announced Grandpop, his eyes lighting up with glee at the prospect of his favourite dish: curry and rice. Kitten and Grandpop would never forget their many years in India but, until rice became available after the war, we had to make do with barley. If rice was hard to come by, so too was curry. That did not deter Puddy who developed an interest in creating curries from scratch, using a collection of exotic spices which she ordered through the post and kept in glass jars in a cupboard in the scullery. The result was always impressive, accompanied by chapattis which Kitten cooked on the girdle, finished off with delicious home-made chutney.

When tea was not appropriate, water accompanied meals. Grandpop was teetotal, but he always stocked drinks in the house, offering whisky or sherry to guests, while brandy provided Kitten with an agreeable substitute for smelling salts.

Surprisingly, maybe, it is not unknown for the

west of Scotland to suffer from drought. There were summers when we had so little rain that the land became parched and it was possible to walk across the Dalvan when the normally soggy moss was so dry that it crunched beneath our feet. Unfortunately this was not always the case, as Puddy knew only too well, having witnessed the death of Iain, her bullock, and he was not the only one. Achaban was surrounded by common grazing, where all the local cattle were free to roam and, despite the warning tufts of bog cotton, it was not unusual for cows to sink into the bog. On one occasion I discovered a cow up to its shoulders in the peat moss near the house. Help was needed urgently and I set off on my bike to alert as many neighbours as possible to come to the aid of the cow. Soon around five or six men had gathered, equipped with ropes. Every effort the cow made to free herself only resulted in her sinking deeper into the morass and she began to tire. The men formed a team, using all their strength and know-how to pull her free with their ropes while one poured water into one of her ears. This looked cruel, but its intention was good. The irritation the cow felt caused her to lurch violently and this sudden effort, along with the ropes, helped to extricate her from the bog. She stood on her feet for a few moments, looking a little puzzled, then calmly walked away as though nothing had happened. If only we could have rescued Iain the same way.

With an excess of water all around us, it was not

easy to convince our visitors of the need for restraint when running a tap. It was only when the water supply faltered that they became aware of the effort which went into maintaining it, and sometimes they became involved in this effort.

CHAPTER NINE

As a little girl, boredom was not an option and, even if I knew the word, I never had the chance to understand its meaning. I was equally unaware that some occupations were gender specific. I enjoyed playing with dolls, and making clothes for them, but I was equally happy to spend time in the cottage, laying out John's old Hornby train set, pushing the engine by hand because the clockwork had long since stopped working. Or I designed and built houses with Minibrix, a forerunner of Lego, but more realistic, with red interlocking rubber bricks and Perspex windows. I also collected Dinky cars with my pocket money, adding them to the Tootsie Toys I inherited from John. There was no heating in the cottage but I never noticed and only went back to the house when hunger reminded me it was time for lunch. Children don't mind weather so I was often indoors when the sun was shining, and outside in the rain. It made no difference although Kitten would call after me 'Don't forget your cardigan!' as I ran out of the house.

Sometimes I took my Dinky cars to a small quarry

nearby, forming single-track roads in the sandy soil for
the cars to follow a trail like the ones I was familiar
with on Mull. Or I played on the Dalvan, floating little
boats in the bog water. I learnt that wherever there
were stinging nettles, a close encounter would result in
red itchy bumps on legs or arms, producing one of the
more painful recollections of childhood. Grandpop's
guidance taught me that a quick glance around would
soon identify a dock leaf nearby which, rubbed on the
spot, would sooth the pain and restore contentment. It
was one of those miracles of nature.

Fortunately I enjoyed rude health but when occasional childhood illness confined me to bed I had the
opportunity to read, even in the morning – an indul-
gence normally considered to be erring towards deca-
dence in a household that clung to Presbyterian values.
My choice of book was always the same in these circumstances: I had no hesitation in asking for a volume
of Arthur Mee's Children's Encyclopaedia. One day,
shortly before I was born, Puddy was mooching in a
second-hand bookshop and happened to notice the
ten matching Morocco-bound volumes. She could not
resist them, and they turned out to be a good invest-
ment. Whenever I had a chance, I browsed through a
volume, chosen at random, page by page, picking up
snippets of information on every subject. It aroused my
latent curiosity in history, astronomy, geography and
poetry, covering both trivial and serious subjects on a
level I could understand while Grandpop would have

approved of its moral and patriotic leanings. But it was a pleasure that was short-lived because days spent in bed were few and far between.

I was usually outdoors and passed a lot of time paddling in the shallows of the loch. I could spend hours just wading up and down in my gumboots towing an old metal float on the end of a string. I called it Old Faithful and even shared the pleasure with a school friend who came to stay. John, perhaps taking pity on me while indulging his boyhood dreams, disappeared into Alistair's room for several weeks, to build a model yacht for my birthday. He used any materials available – a hull made from cardboard, a mast from a walking stick, and sails from an old damask tablecloth. A year or so later he was even more ambitious, building a model liner, with a cardboard hull, and a soup tin funnel. I launched her with due ceremony, and watched while her clockwork engine propelled her through the water – no need for string.

In hot weather, I shared my enjoyment of the loch with the cattle which paddled to cool their feet. It was quite evident from the number of cow-pats on the bed of the loch that the cows spent a lot of time there. It never bothered me that this was our water supply.

At its best, a simple turn of the tap released hot or cold water as needed, its dark colour assuredly due to peat and not cow-pats. The method of transferring it from loch to basin was simple enough – the electric generator ran a pump that drew the water out of the loch and up to tanks in the loft. In fact it relied on several different processes, any one of which could fail. The price of petrol was low when the generator was first installed, but it steadily rose to a dizzy five shillings a gallon (25p in new money) and no-one could ignore Grandpop's tut-tutting as each bill arrived. So Kitten and Puddy agreed to run the engine only on the days when it was required to operate the pump. This is why we seldom enjoyed the benefits of electric light, but spent much of our time, especially in winter, huddled in the little morning-room by the light of oil lamps.

Grandpop had devised a clever method of gauging the level of the water in the two huge tanks in the loft. A float in one of the tanks was attached to a rod which dropped through the loft floor to the linen cupboard beneath. At the bottom end of the rod, a gauge (recognisable as a piece of Meccano) hung against marks on the wall, indicating the water level in the tank above. It was an ingenious contraption but it did not prevent water from overflowing. For that, human intervention was required. It was up to one of us to check the gauge and this was a job I was well equipped to do – running up and down stairs at intervals to check the gauge against the marks on the linen cupboard wall. When it met a certain level, it was time to turn the pump off.

The pump was down by the loch, occupying its own little shed. So long as the electric engine was running, a red button in the lobby beside the kitchen operated the pump. If all went well, the water was raised from the loch and started to flow into the tanks. Once the gauge reached the correct level, we were assured of enough water to keep us going for two or three days, so long as we were prudent with its use. This meant never running a tap before putting the plug in the basin; never emptying the dishwater down the plughole until every item had been washed. These habits became so deeply ingrained that I still find it hard to wash anything, including myself, under a running tap. Conversely, a shower would have saved valuable water, but this was a luxury too much and when scrupulous cleansing was necessary, or a good wallow to relax tired limbs, we filled the bath. It is perfectly possible to strip wash thoroughly so I have to confess that we did not often feel the need for a bath, and when we did, it became quite a ritual. For one thing, the bathroom, on the north side of the house, was freezing cold in winter. So we lit an oil heater about half an hour before the anticipated bathing time. Then the bath was large, and the water ran slowly, so we had to turn the tap on well in advance. The hot water in the chill of the room created a steamy haze as we entered, almost snuffing out the paraffin heater through lack of oxygen. Although we were accustomed to it, the colour of the water was not to everybody's taste. It was like bathing in strong tea, but it was so soft that a bar of soap readily created bubbles when swished around for a moment or two. This was all possible when the pump worked properly.

It did not always run so easily. Sometimes it was only

able to bring the water up the hill, but not up to the loft. Occasionally it seized up altogether. Grandpop would take his box of tools, tins of grease, cans of oil and a bundle of grubby cloths down to the little shed by the loch. Despite a back bent by arthritis, he often spent hours lying on the rough grass, his hands wrestling with the mechanism, persuading it to work. Whistling an inane little tune between his teeth, he plodded up and down the drive between engine and pump, until he had a reaction. Or not. If the pump only succeeded in raising the water to the house, another plan of action was needed and this could involve our guests.

It required manpower to raise water to the tanks and the old hand-pump in the scullery was brought into use. As the only child in a family of strong adults, I was not expected to take an equal turn at the pump, but I often had a go for fun. It was hard work to fill the tanks to a safe level – enough to keep the boiler happy.

Despite Grandpop's constant care and attention, the pump sometimes seized up completely. Then there was no alternative but to summon a mechanic from Tobermory or the mainland. This happened a number of times but on one occasion a man came from Oban by the *King George V* and we agreed to meet him at the jetty. Now it so happened that Florrie was suffering from one of her maladies so we harnessed Corrie to the dog-cart and set off down to Fionnphort to meet the ferry. The mechanic duly arrived but took one look at Corrie and the dog-cart and flatly refused to accept a lift, preferring to walk the mile or so, while allowing us to carry his tools and a replacement pump in the trap. Having restored our water supply, the poor man had no choice but to spend the night with us, for there was nowhere else to stay, but he left on the mail bus early next morning to avoid any chance of having to accept a lift in the dog-cart.

Even when the pump failed, we still had a water supply. Cool clear water came from a tap in the scullery attached to a tank outside which collected rainwater from the scullery roof. This was our drinking water. Without the taint of peat and iron, its clarity made a much more agreeable appearance than the water from the loch but I suspect that a microscope would have revealed a disturbing level of activity within its depths. A simple filter trapped dead leaves and insects but the water was never purified or chlorinated. During the First World War Grandpop was a medical officer in Mesopotamia (present-day Iraq) and knew only too well the perils of bad drinking water. He devised a simple but successful method of chlorinating water for use by the troops which was ultimately adopted by all the units, and his papers appeared in the *British Medical Journal*. Despite this, I cannot remember ever seeing our tank drained or cleaned and, so far as I am aware, Grandpop did not apply much concern to our drinking water from the scullery roof.

When the water supply from the loch failed, we used this drinking water for washing ourselves. We filled enamel ewers and carried them upstairs at bedtime, for use in our basins, keeping half the water ready for the following morning. As anyone who has gone camping will know, it is amazing how little water is necessary for a good scrub and the cold water wash was certainly invigorating.

To avoid crossing the landing to that chilly bathroom in the middle of the night, we kept 'poe-ys', or chamber pots, under our beds or in a side cupboard, emptying them discreetly during the day, as generations had done before. We were less squeamish in those days.

As I said before, droughts can and do occur even on the west coast of Scotland and when this coincided with a breakdown in our water supply, and the rain-water tank threatened to run dry, there was only one other option left: the well. There were two wells down by the loch. One attracted the frog population and every year I enjoyed dredging it for tadpoles. The other provided our emergency water supply but it had to be carried up to the house in buckets.

I soon discovered that there was no point filling my gaily painted beach bucket to the rim. No matter how careful I was, some of the precious liquid slurped over the edge as I tottered up the hill towards the house, but I was always made to feel my small contribution was valuable.

Despite these occasional setbacks, our water supply was fairly reliable but we dreamt of some distant day when we would be put on 'the mains'. In anticipation of this, Grandpop once again used the skills he had exploited during the First World War. He sketched a simple plan that, in theory, could provide the whole district with water from the loch. He suggested a pump close to the loch that could pipe water to a holding tank on Tormore. From here it could be released using gravity through pipes to all the households. He sent his sketch to the local authority, expecting it to be lost forever on some dusty shelf. For once, he was wrong. Within a few years, a government scheme for the supply of water to outlandish places was put into action and Grandpop's plans were selected simply because they were there. The Royal Engineers, requiring a task to fulfil as an exercise, were deployed to undertake the work.

The new water supply was very welcome, but although it was chlorinated, the colour had not improved. Even though the local cattle were restricted from wading near the deep entry point of the new pipe, the water was still a dark peaty brown.

So we continued to drink the clear – if lively – rainwater from the scullery roof.

CHAPTER TEN

Nicholas understood Grandpop's concern for him when the weather was wild, but he resented being kept indoors at night. His whiskers bristled and his tail waved in a none too subtle display of the feral side of his character. He was well known throughout the neighbourhood and was sometimes away for nights at a time, even weeks. But he would eventually return, often to be found in the company of Corrie, nestling contentedly on her shoulder, or he slipped into the engine house when the generator was off. He enjoyed the residual heat, and the warmth of the old red hospital blanket that Grandpop thoughtfully left for his comfort. But whenever possible, he came into the house during the day. He curled up on the little square stool in the morning-room, to sleep soundly after a night spent hunting – or out on the tiles.

It has to be admitted that Puddy had very little success with crops despite all the effort she put into cultivating them, and the Big Park, with its pale grass, yielded a very sparse crop of hay. The little stack we produced with so much effort had to be supplemented so Puddy ordered a ton of hay in preparation for each winter. The hay arrived on a lorry but the twenty bales, each weighing a hundredweight, had to be manhandled into the barn, an arduous task, because the lorry could not be brought close to the entrance of the barn. But help was at hand. Puddy struck lucky at a local displenishing sale where a job lot of farm implements included a solid iron porter's trolley on two wheels. It proved to be invaluable for carting all manner of heavy goods, from bales of hay to refrigerators, and I have it to this day. We called it 'the trundler' and it made short work of moving the hay into the barn where we stacked it neatly ready for the winter. The hay filled one wall of the barn and chinks between the bales made a cosy home for the progeny of Nicholas, whose mothers instinctively knew what was best for their young. We would climb to the top of the stack and, sitting in silence, our patience would be rewarded as each kitten tentatively emerged, blinking, into the subdued light of the barn. We watched their antics with delight as they played their games, learning to hover and pounce, chase and catch. One day these skills would stand them in good stead when their need to hunt became serious. Cute though they were, these kittens would never find their way into the house or by the hearth so they must learn to feed themselves. Although we discouraged them, each season a number collected at the back of the house, scrounging for scraps. They became known as 'the window-sill cats', dancing on the ledge outside the kitchen window. We sometimes took pity on them, but generally tried to avoid attracting them – at one point we counted twenty-seven – which Nicholas himself acknowledged was too much of a good thing. Besides, there were plenty of rats and mice and rabbits around and we really wanted to encourage them to hunt for their own food.

While the cat population increased, so the number of mice and rats declined. This was comforting, for the occasional sound of scuttling behind the skirting boards and across the rafters could not be ignored. Rats were in occupation. They came into the house during harvest time and we called them the 'Clog Dancers' for the noise they made. They were enormous – the size of baby rabbits – and they were very bold. I once saw one sitting up on the boiler bracket in the scullery, watching Kitten at the sink. I called her away urgently and shut the door firmly, hoping it would find its own way out. The legendary prowess of Nicholas was repeated generation after generation although few could match his ability to kill rabbits.

Until the Aga and its adjoining boiler were installed, the kitchen was dominated by a huge black range with an oven set in beside the grate. It gave a glow of comfort but needed constant stoking. In the scullery a squat little boiler skulked in the corner. 'Ideal' by name, but not by nature, this monstrosity awaited the attention of Puddy who shovelled coke into its greedy belly at frequent intervals throughout the day. Its voracious appetite rewarded us with nothing more than a copper cylinder full of hot water, perched on a bracket above the boiler.

During the summer months the range gave off too much heat and consumed too much coal. So Kitten used an oil cooker in the scullery instead. It consisted of a metal frame enclosing three burners fed by a large glass bottle filled with paraffin, attached to one side. A separate portable oven was placed over two of the burners so that Kitten could roast and bake while simmering soup on the third burner. It was an antediluvian arrangement but it worked and, so far as I recall, it did not result in many cooking disasters.

By the early 1950s some space was lost in the kitchen when an Aga and Agamatic boiler replaced the old range. The Agamatic swallowed up all manner of stuff that would otherwise be thrown away. Potato peelings went into the hen bucket while Carla, being a spaniel, was only too happy to eat all our leftovers. There was no rubbish collection so we had to burn or bury everything else that was not edible. There was a patch outside the back gate where Grandpop supervised bonfires for large items such as cardboard boxes and old magazines. And once in a while Wee Sandy came to dig a pit nearby for tin cans and suchlike. Some day in the future, archaeologists will discover a trench full of jars and tins and wonder what we did with so much Marmite. The nook once occupied by the 'Ideal' boiler became the perfect alcove for Carla's bed, although she used it only at night, preferring to be wherever Puddy was at all other times.

The rest of the rooms were heated by open fires fed with coal. The coal came to Bunessan on a puffer from Glasgow, then by lorry. It was heaped in a big pile beside the garage before we transferred it by bucket or barrow to the coalhouse. This was conveniently within the back porch so we could keep warm and dry when filling the coal hods and scuttles during the dark winter months.

Shipping charges always added to the expense of living on an island but sometimes there were unexpected benefits. Good quality anthracite was very dense so, weight for weight, it took up less space in a ship's hold than the lighter coke. Space on a ship is at a premium, but because of this, anthracite was much better value. Bearing this in mind, Courtier stoves, using anthracite, were installed in the dining room and two of the bedrooms. They had little doors that opened to reveal the warm glow of the fire inside and they were permanently lit throughout the winter months. I very much doubt if these would be permitted in bedrooms now without proper ventilation, but I'm glad to say that no-one succumbed to the fumes during the night and their warmth ensured that the chill winter mornings were bearable.

Wood burners were not an option in those days. Wood was not available locally and it would be many years before the new timber plantations reached maturity. However, we were surrounded by peat moss: we had only to look at the Dalvan at the back of the house. The long ridges of the peat hags, the channels of water where I floated walnut boats, or studied water-boatmen, showed that peat had been dug here for many generations. Although we never relied on peat, we used it to supplement our coal supply, but providing enough peat to last us the winter was a long and labour-intensive process.

First, the fibrous top layer of earth, including the tough roots of heather and bog myrtle, had to be stripped away and Wee Sandy sometimes came to do this most arduous task. Then we cut each peat using a special L-shaped spade, or peat knife, which varied in shape from place to place, fashioned by the local blacksmith. At its best, the oily bog water made it easy to cut – like slicing through a rich suet pudding, dense but moist. Every so often we came across clear evidence that, where there were now moors, there had once been great forests. We dug up twisted roots or branches, well preserved by the lack of oxygen in the bog. It was these trees, along with other compost material, that caused the peat bogs to form in the first place. Our ancestors long ago had used the timber for building material, or fuel, or to clear the land by burning for cultivation or livestock. Nothing around us was as nature intended.

Each peat was square cut and long and, as they were very soggy, we laid them side by side on the bank to dry in the sun. They were very dark to begin with but over the next few weeks, we turned them until they began to pale. We then stood each peat on end to form stooks of three or four that allowed the wind to blow through them to help the drying process. Contrary to general belief, it doesn't rain all the time on the west coast of Scotland and the low-lying land is drier than many inland areas but, without trees, it is very exposed, so it is one of the windiest inhabited places in the world. The sun and the wind together caused the peats to dry.

Working out on the moor had its attractions. There was a feast of nature all around us, from the broad sky above, with skylarks trilling their song of joy, the chirping of grasshoppers hiding in the heather, the fluttering of butterflies and buzzing of bees. And there was the mysterious low whirring of snipe that could be heard but seldom seen. Peaceful it was not, but those sounds filled the heart with the calm pleasure of knowing that all was right with the world.

We left the peat for two or three weeks before checking them again, rearranging them into larger stooks until they were brittle and crumbly to the touch. It was time to bring them home.

One day Puddy was making stooks when she picked up a peat and promptly yelped. She noticed the tail of a snake sticking out of one end. At the other, she recognised the distinctive marks on the head of an adder, and promptly dropped the peat. Adders, the only poisonous snake in the British Isles, would probably only harm if under threat, but Puddy didn't wait to test this theory. Knowing how much time I spent on my own out in the open, Grandpop once preserved a dead adder in a jar for reference, so that I knew what to avoid if I ever encountered one. Grass snakes and lizards were fairly common. Apart from the coiled-up snake in a jar, I never knowingly met an adder.

Outnumbering vipers by the million, midges are the worst scourge of the Highlands. These tiny terrorists of the tourism industry, which come out in droves from June to September, have ruined many a holiday but young blood does not appear to appeal to them and they never bothered me as a child. On the other hand, large horseflies, known as clegs, were very partial to Grandpop, softly landing on his arms or legs. He never noticed until their bite caused an irritating wheal on his skin. Nicholas often came home from hunting expeditions covered in ticks. Every evening Grandpop checked his coat and removed their bloated bodies with a skilful twist of finger and thumb, ensuring their heads were not left behind.

The process of bringing the peat home conveniently came during the school holidays so there were plenty of helping hands. They were needed. Although each peat was now light and airy, a creel or sack of peats was heavy. We carried them on our backs, which was hard work, so we welcomed any additional helper. Puddy bought a pair of panniers for Corrie who had no difficulty in walking across the bog, knowing instinctively where the dangerous places were. With her panniers filled with peat, she could carry the load of several people, and she greatly reduced our toil.

Finally, we built a peat stack outside the back door. Throughout the neighbourhood, perfectly formed peat stacks displayed the skill of their owners. Some of them, with rounded corners and sloping roofs, looked the image of the adjoining croft cottages. They withstood all the winter storms could toss at them, repelling both wind and rain. Try as we did, we could never emulate the best peat stacks in the district. Nowadays you are more likely to see metal tanks by the back door, holding oil for heating.

Because it burned so fast, we used peat in addition to coal. Peat on its own burns to a very fine ash with a tendency to form a dusty film over everything, but it has one useful quality. By smothering the embers of an open fire with peat ash, it can be left all night and revived the following morning. The greatest benefit was the wonderful warm aroma that invaded the house, and the sweet scent of peat, curling from so many chimneys, permeated the air of the whole district.

The same could not be said for the cumbersome and rather inefficient oil-filled radiator that lived in the hall. It tended to emit smoky fumes that wafted up to the landing but without it the hall would have been bitterly cold. Portable black paraffin heaters boosted the warmth during the depth of winter wherever they were needed.

The crisp chill of a winter evening was in stark

contrast with the warmth within the house. The combined scent of peat and paraffin diffused the air upon entering the hall but, despite all the best efforts of the various heat sources, there were some areas of the house best avoided. I have already mentioned the bathroom, where it was essential to light an oil heater well in advance of a bath. My little bedroom, with a window facing east, also required a portable oil heater for there was no fireplace. The study beyond the dining room was always cold – and that was where one of the first telephones in the district had been installed.

It was one of those old-fashioned phones with the mouthpiece at the top of a tall stalk. When not in use, the hearing part was clipped to the stalk, a twisted flex enabling it to reach the ear while making a call. Telephone calls were few because Grandpop thought they were an extravagant form of communication. While local calls could be dialled direct, all others went through the exchange at Lochdonhead, near Craignure, manned by Morag who was always there, morning, noon and night. Many a story was told of Morag's powers but chief among them was her knowledge of everyone's whereabouts on the island at any given time. If Kitten wanted to speak to Mrs So-and-So, Morag could direct the call to whatever house Mrs So-and-So was visiting.

Not all calls were within the island. When Margie was in London, respecting Grandpop's dislike of telephone bills, she made a weekly trunk call home that involved a long process linking several exchanges between London and Fionnphort. Although known locally as 'Finnafort', Kitten was born and lived in old Fionnphort House and always pronounced it 'Fewn-fort' so Margie spelt the name to the switchboard girl 'F for Freddy – I – O – double N for Nelly' to avoid confusion but even then the call sometimes ended up somewhere else. If the lines were busy, as they often were at the weekend, she had to book the call in advance. Once through, the conversation followed the same course. 'What's the weather like?' followed by 'Can you hear me?' Every three minutes a series of pips warned that the bill was mounting. More than three sets of pips threatened to set off Grandpop's grumbles, even when he wasn't footing the bill. More than five and he was almost apoplectic. As a result I never formed a close relationship with telephones and dislike them to this day.

In any case, unless there was something serious to be discussed, no-one spent more time than necessary in the study. It was too fiendishly cold.

CHAPTER ELEVEN

While avoiding the coldest rooms of the house whenever possible, we generally congregated in the areas
of greatest warmth – in the cosy little morning-room,
or the kitchen. Puddy could usually be found draped
over the Aga, sipping soup from the ladle, ostensibly
tasting it, but Nicholas had no hesitation in describing
this activity as stealing. Knowing the hotspots was easy
enough for the family; our guests may not have found it
so simple. It is a fact about other people's houses – they
are invariably cold – so our luckless visitors had to find
their own levels of comfort. We could not, in fairness,
apply to our guests the old saying that fish and visitors
smell after three days. By the time they had reached us,
they needed to stay long enough to make their journey
worthwhile. There were plenty of things for them to
do, and places to visit, so sightseeing filled much of
the time.

There was never any doubt about the first trip. 'We'll
take you to Iona on the first good day,' Kitten would
say firmly, and no-one ever argued with her. The result
was that, throughout my childhood, I thought Iona

always basked in sunshine. It was like a Mediterranean island – an emerald gem, with silver sands, surrounded by a sapphire sea. Yet this glorious island was just a short drive and a ferry trip away.

Dan and his brother Angie provided the ferry service, running white motorboats back and forth across the narrow Sound of Iona that divided Mull from the sacred isle. The ferry left from the jetty at Fionnphort where the pink granite rocks added a semi-precious facet to the gem-like qualities of the scene. Fionnphort means 'white port', and a huge cleft rock sits in the middle of the sandy bay. Various stories are told about how this great granite boulder came to be split. Records state that the Duke of Argyll intervened when quarrymen split it with the idea of breaking it up some time around 1870. It bears just one borehole and Margie once told me that her grandfather blew it up as a surprise for her fourth birthday. Remembering that he was quite capable of organising this, and that he famously had a wicked sense of humour, I like her story although I confess it is somewhat dubious. It would have been 1914, a very sensitive time to blow up a giant boulder just for fun. Whichever story is true, there is little doubt that my great-grandfather, who had worked at the quarry from an early age before taking over as manager in 1875, probably had something to do with it. And I confess to having a somewhat nefarious pride in this.

When crossing the Sound, I preferred the smaller of

the two ferry boats. It was so low that we could hang over the side and trail our fingers in the cool water. With one hand on the tiller, and puffing a pipe from the corner of his mouth, Dan steered a varying course across the Sound to avoid the sandbanks that shifted in response to powerful currents. The pellucid waters astonished visitors. The sun shone so brightly through the clear water that sparkles of shimmering light reflected off the pattern of ripples formed in the white sand of the seabed. Contrasting dark fronds of seaweed swirled rhythmically with the movement of the waves.

As the boat approached the jetty, the Abbey appeared, square and solid, behind the row of little houses that formed the village, their gardens leading down to the water's edge. Once ashore, we walked up to the Nunnery, where the ruins enclosed an untamed but tranquil garden filled with rambling roses. From there we passed Maclean's Cross and the manse and parish church designed by Thomas Telford. We then explored the Relig Oran where the Ridge of Kings was still in place, marked out by low railings. It was thought to contain the remains of Scottish and Norwegian kings, including Macbeth. The intricately decorated grave slabs, which were arranged in a row, have since been removed for preservation in the restored Infir-mary Museum.

Kitten liked to join us on visits to Iona. It was a step back in time for her to see the tall granite obelisk near the west wall that marked the graves of her parents.

(Many years later John Smith was laid to rest alongside this wall. His untimely death as leader of the Labour Party was greatly lamented even by those of a different political persuasion.) Nearby, the ruins of St Oran's Chapel reminded us that St Columba was not the gentle saint his name 'the dove' implied. The story was told that his followers could not complete the building of this chapel unless a live man was buried beneath the foundations. Oran duly volunteered, and sometime later, after the building was finished, Columba ordered Oran's body to be recovered. Not only was Oran found to be alive, but he declared that neither heaven nor hell existed, whereupon Columba commanded that he be reburied forthwith! The present chapel dates from 1200, long after Columba's time, and has since been restored.

From here it was a short walk to the Abbey where three Celtic crosses guarded the entrance. Excavators had not yet discovered the Street of the Dead which leads from the Relig Oran to the Abbey. Kitten remembered the Abbey in ruins before it was rebuilt by the 8th Duke of Argyll who gave it to the Church of Scotland on condition that it should be used by all Christian denominations. His grand memorial, alongside his wife, awed me as a child, their stark marble figures lying behind a wrought-iron gate in a side aisle. Ina was his third wife and she was buried in Iona, so her marble figure wears a coronet on her head, while the Duke's coronet lies at his feet, to show that he was buried elsewhere, a curious but interesting fact.

The Abbey was built mainly of granite, brought from Mull, and the interior was a beautiful mellow shade of pink, lit by shafts of light coming through the clear glass windows. Although the Abbey Church was complete, it was surrounded by ruins. The cloisters, refectory, dormitory and chapels were all in need of restoration. Dr George MacLeod formed the Iona Community in 1938 to restore the buildings around the Abbey using the labour of unemployed craftsmen from his parish in Glasgow, which was suffering severe hardship during the Depression. (Although a baronet in his own right, George, as he was known by everyone, did not accept a title until he was elevated, as Lord MacLeod of Fuinary, to the House of Lords in 1967.)

It was fascinating to watch building methods that could not have changed since medieval times for, of course, there was no electricity. Wheelbarrows were used to transport the huge stones that were raised by ropes and pulleys to rebuild the cloister walls. Skilled stonemasons carved intricate designs on corbels and capitals with hammer and chisel under the watchful gaze of visitors.

George was a commanding figure with a resonant, but unmistakably Scottish voice. His experience in the First World War, which rewarded his bravery on the battlefield with a Military Cross, converted him to pacifism. He had a ready wit and strong views, many of them political, which met with disapproval, not least from Nicholas, but he was a good friend to the family and often dropped in at Achaban when passing through Mull. We sometimes met him at the Abbey where he was always prepared to spend time with visitors. When the Refectory was newly restored, he proudly showed us round and told of the miracle that allowed the completion of the roof, using timber donated by Norway in reparation for Viking raids so many centuries before. He was a fine orator and a consoling counsellor. I happened to be with a friend who needed reassurance about marrying a divorced man. When asked if the Lord would approve, George thought for a moment, before giving a carefully measured reply: 'The good Lord accepts only one marriage.' He paused briefly. 'But it needn't necessarily be the first!' While not entirely biblical, this utterance was certainly reassuring to my friend and counted for much, coming from a truly charismatic man of God.

After exploring the Abbey we climbed the little mound close to the west door where we settled on the grassy bank, unwrapped our sandwiches, and opened a Thermos flask. From here we could watch visitors flocking off the *King George V* making their way towards the Abbey while we enjoyed our picnic in the sun. It would be some years before this mound was excavated and declared to be of sacred significance, identified as Tor Abb, the site of St Columba's cell.

St Columba came to Iona in the sixth century but the rocks of the island are among the oldest in the world and it is well worth exploring. Despite the thousands of people who visit Iona each summer, it is amazing how they disperse and there are always quiet places to be found. A pleasant walk was more likely to be disturbed by the croak of corncrakes or bleat of sheep separated from their lambs. We sometimes dropped in on cousins who lived in a tiny cottage near the crest of the road leading to the machair on the west coast. The whitewashed walls and low thatched roof contained a snug interior with seats arranged around a small black stove. During the course of an hour or so we listened to Cousin Johnnie's stories of his father, a great Gaelic scholar, while Cousin Margaret dispensed an astonishing succession of scones and pancakes from the heat of the little stove. We once made a special visit to admire their new baby who cooed and gurgled in a basket under the protective care of a couple of collie dogs. Johnnie was in the process of building a new house nearby. Before the ubiquitous kit houses became available, and transport improved, building materials had to be ordered separately and shipped to the island by puffers. This would take a long time but the new house would in future years replace the small but cosy but'n'ben.

At other times we walked to the north end of the island, with its dazzling white beaches, natural sand dunes and brilliant green grass, grazed by contented fluffy sheep. The great headland of Burg, on Mull, formed the backdrop with the pink granite of Tormore just across the water. Little wonder that this landscape

inspired the Scottish Colourists of the 1920s and 30s –
Francis Cadell and Samuel Peploe among others. Their
paintings are to be found in great art galleries, and just
to look at one recalls the glorious natural beauty in the
translucent light of the islands.

Every week George led a pilgrimage around the
island when a group followed him across the machair,
strewn with tiny sweet-scented flowers, on the west
side, to the green marble quarry, and the bay where
Columba and his twelve followers first landed in
563 AD, having established that they could no longer
see Ireland, from which he was allegedly banned. The
tour ended on the top of Dun I, Iona's highest hill
– little more than 300 ft, but in perfect proportion
to the size of the island, which is three miles by one.
The view from the top was stunning – to the west, the
wide Atlantic, non-stop to Canada, while Mull and its
offshore islands embraced the other side. To the south
was Dubh Artach Lighthouse, and to the north, the
lofty peaks of the Isle of Rum formed a ragged edge to
the horizon.

Before the dormitories were built, temporary
buildings were erected to house members of the Community. The row of wooden cabins resembled a train
and acquired the name amongst locals of 'The Rome
Express', a facetious reference to the candles which
lit the Abbey and raised Presbyterian eyebrows. John
stayed here when he worked with the Community,
digging up stones and cutting grass. Later, I spent odd

nights as a guest of the Community although I confess I was more interested in the social life, which included dances in the village hall.

We sometimes attended services in the Abbey, which took place frequently throughout the summer. Singing was accompanied by the distinctive sound of a grand piano, for there was no organ. One special occasion was to see the christening of our baby cousin who bellowed so lustily during the service that it was almost impossible to hear George's words while he marked the sign of the cross with water from the beautifully ornamented baptismal font by the west door.

We did not always have to go to the Abbey to hear George preach. Every August the BBC broadcast a Sunday service directly from the Abbey and we listened to it on the wireless. As Iona had no electricity, all the equipment, including generators, had to be ferried ashore and manhandled to the Abbey for this annual occasion. There were no cars on the island and only a few rudimentary tractors. It must have been a daunting undertaking. The service always started with the steady toll of the Abbey bell to summon the congregation and I enjoyed popping outside Achaban to listen to the bell as it rang across the water, following closely behind its sonorous 'bong' on the radio's airwaves. The speed of sound needed no further explanation.

Contrary to my beliefs as a child, the ferocity of the gales that beat upon the Ross of Mull, lashing the coast and bending the trees, did not mystically avoid

Iona. Although we so often saw it on balmy days, when sunshine emphasised the rich palette of colours, Iona's landscape, almost devoid of trees, proved that it bore the brunt of the full blast of the Atlantic. When it wasn't windy, a dank shroud often hung over the island, clothing it entirely and erasing it from sight. At other times, drought parched the land, adding severe water shortage to a scanty supply at the best of times. This could cause problems when the resident population was joined by visitors during the summer and notices appeared entreating 'Stink or Swim!'. Rainfall restored the balance on which the green of the grass relied.

Iona leaves a lasting impression on everyone who goes there. Some experience peace, others a heightened awareness of the world around them. When Doctor Johnson visited Iona in 1773 he commented: 'That man is little to be envied . . . whose piety would not grow warmer among the ruins of Iona.' Nicholas could not have put it better.

CHAPTER TWELVE

Most of our visitors wanted to see as much of the island as possible during their stay and that invariably involved a long car drive, for the north of Mull is very different from the south. I was ten years old before I went to Tobermory for the first time as all our connections were with Oban, despite the arduous journey there and back. Puddy had a friend to stay so a trip to the north end of the island gave us a good excuse for a day out.

We set off in Florrie, with me in the back, and took the left-hand fork in the road at Kinloch. It was August, and Glen Seilisdeir – the glen of irises – should have been renamed Glen Fraoch – the glen of heather – for the hills were ablaze with purple. The road took us up to the dramatic view, looking towards the Treshnish Isles, before leading us down through a series of tight bends towards the dangerous rocks at Gribun. It was at this precise moment that Florrie chose to snap her brakes. Puddy had no option but to carry on, for she couldn't stop Florrie. It happened that it was the day of the Salen Show, the island's largest agricultural show, so there was far more traffic on the road than usual, and all of it seemed to be coming in the opposite direction. This is very alarming on a single-track road, with long intervals between passing places. When cars approached ahead of us, Puddy used the handbrake and tootled the horn at the same time. It was remarkable – and fortunate – how quickly the other drivers reacted to the situation, sliding as far to their left as they dared without falling into the ditch. I think the aim of our journey was to go to the show, but instead Puddy drove to Tobermory to find one of the few garages on the island able to repair Florrie's brakes. I really don't remember much about Tobermory in those days. It was long before it became famous for its brightly painted multicoloured houses, and long before the television show *Balamory* and a book called *The Tobermory Cat* drew flocks of families with young children to see the place for themselves.

It would be three or four years before I returned to Tobermory at the invitation of an old friend of the family whose large house overlooked the bay. She invited Puddy and me to lunch and thoughtfully arranged a fishing trip for me to while away the afternoon. She introduced me to a girl and two boys, sharing two boats between us. Needless to say, the boys went in one boat, leaving me with the girl in the other. Despite the fact that I had grown up with a permanent view of our loch, we never had a boat, and I had never tried rowing – or fishing for that matter. This was to change as a result of that one afternoon in Tobermory Bay. The girl rowed out to the centre of the bay and cast a fishing line overboard. The boys did likewise and before long they were hauling in mackerel by the dozen while we only caught three. Then she offered me the oars. Within minutes I discovered the pleasure of controlling the direction of the boat, while skimming smoothly through the water.

I was hooked – but by rowing, not fishing. When we returned home, I talked about nothing else. No-one took any notice of me except Grandpop who listened patiently, tut-tutted occasionally and puffed on his pipe thoughtfully, but offered no solution.

Each week we received the *Oban Times*, which must claim to be one of the most widely distributed local papers anywhere, due to the scattering of Highlanders and Islanders to the four corners of the earth (a concept Nicholas once questioned, noting that the world is round). The *Oban Times* reported anything and everything of interest throughout the area extending from the Outer Hebrides to the very heart of Glasgow, where so many Gaels stayed during their working lives.

The reports were interesting or amusing in about equal measure: Highland Games, agricultural shows, sales of work. From photographs of pupils attending school for the first time, to couples celebrating their diamond weddings, all aspects of human life were represented within its pages. Personal messages, placed with genuine affection by grieving relatives, sometimes provoked a wry smile. But the advertisements, appearing as an unclassified and haphazard list, were always a source of curiosity. They ranged from 'Heifer for sale' through 'Wanted: wheelbarrow' to the cryptic 'Lost: one kilt somewhere in Glen More' (truly!), demanding, but not providing, an explanation.

I had my thoughts on only one thing. As the result of my recent birthday, I had some spare money and with this in mind, I scanned the column in search of a boat for sale. By chance, after just a couple of weeks, I saw exactly what I was looking for. The advertisement read 'For sale: 12ft flat-bottom dinghy. Delivery by arrangement.' I responded at once to the box number and received a reply from a man who lived in Applecross on the mainland which, at that time, was even more remote than we were on the Ross of Mull. An exchange of correspondence followed in which he explained that he had built the boat himself and was now building another, bigger and better. He offered the dinghy for £20, a sum that far exceeded the money I had acquired and so, with deep regret, I wrote to decline his offer. It was the end of the holidays, and I returned to school for the autumn term, a new class, and a season of hockey. With so much to keep me occupied, the boat became a distant dream.

I had quite forgotten this episode by the time the Christmas holidays came. The whole family were home, and that included Margie with Lottie, her poodle, which she had acquired a couple of years before and had become her closest companion. Nicholas told of his first encounter with Lottie, when he admitted to his shame that he spat and arched his back at her, never having seen such a strange animal before. He later conceded that she was a most amiable creature and quoted her claim that there were many different animals in the world including 'dogs and cats and poodles and mice' to emphasise the point that she considered poodles were a separate species, and who could disagree?

He probably did not know that I was one of the first people to meet her. I was staying with Margie in London when we went to Paddington Station to greet Lottie off the train from Shrewsbury. She was a pathetic and bedraggled little creature, having suffered badly from travel sickness, and within an hour of her arrival Margie had no option but to give her a good bath, not normally recommended for a young puppy. She soon recovered from her ordeal, and once her coat had fluffed up, she looked less like a rat and more like a lamb.

She was born in the year of the Coronation and her Kennel Club name, Salote, was after the hugely popular Queen of Tonga. Famously, throughout the procession to Westminster Abbey, in pouring rain, Queen Salote's generous smile beamed from the carriage she shared with the diminutive Sultan of Kelantan. (You may not know that Kelantan is a state in Malaysia. I had to look it up.) Not only large, she was unusually tall, well over six feet, and the story was told that, when a reporter asked who her companion in the carriage was, the reply came: 'her dinner!'

I saw her for myself. It was half term and, along with thousands of others, I spent the night on the pavement in The Mall with Puddy and John for company. Margie came to dispense sandwiches before returning to the comfort of her flat nearby where she settled comfortably to watch the event on television. While we listened to the Coronation service on loudspeakers attached to trees in the Mall, Kitten, accompanied by Grandpop, climbed Tormore, the hill behind Fionnphort. When they reached the top, Kitten set light to the bonfire. It was fittingly within yards of the house where she was born, and it was one of many beacons around the British Isles celebrating this great royal occasion. The local people had gone to great trouble to collect the material and carry it up the hill. The lighting of that bonfire was a simple act which connected the vast crowds in London with one of the smallest communities in Britain, a fact which would not fail to appeal to Nicholas.

But to return to Christmas Eve: as usual, everyone had secrets to keep from everyone else and I did not notice that the adults were being unduly furtive. At one point they actively excluded me from some ploy which Puddy maintained could only be done outside and didn't require my help. Christmas morning followed the same routine as always except that this time Puddy made the tea for everyone and brought it up to Kitten and Grandpop's room. My pillowcase was not so full as usual. As I grew older, I noticed that my presents were diminishing in size but increasing in value. It was to be expected. So I was not surprised when I finished unwrapping my presents before everyone else.

Then Grandpop said, 'It's time to draw the curtains back; it must be light enough outside.' I should explain that the days were very short around midwinter and it was barely light before nine a.m. What is more, unless Christmas Day fell on a Sunday, there would be no church, so we were not in any hurry. 'Let Fionna do it,' Kitten instructed from the comfort of her bed.

I duly pulled the curtains back and glanced outside. And then I looked again, unable at first to comprehend what my eyes were seeing. There on the lawn lay my boat! I knew it was mine because it answered exactly the description of my nice man in Applecross. I soon discovered that Grandpop had taken up the correspondence on my behalf and arranged for the boat to be delivered by Archie-the-Carrier. Somehow the family had hidden it from view during the first three or four days of the holiday, and dragged it round to the lawn under the cover of darkness.

I spent the next few days staring through the window at my boat, and at the loch, for it was too wild to put the boat in the water. I had to be patient, for it was several days before the wind abated and the waves settled down. I say 'my boat' for, rather like my bicycle, I was in complete charge of it, unlike Corrie who relied on Puddy to look after her most of the time. The difference of course was that the boat and the bicycle could manage perfectly well without me during the school term, whereas Corrie couldn't. Also, Corrie had work to do and neither my bike or my boat contributed much to the running of the household.

It was not until the spring and summer holidays that I had a chance to use the boat in earnest. Legend told that the largest island, the one at the far end of the loch, was once inhabited by a hermit and that stepping stones beneath the water linked it to the shore. Another claimed that the smallest island, which was close by, and almost disappeared below water level after heavy rainfall, was man-made. If that was the case, it posed the question, why would anyone bother to wade out into the water and pile earth into a mound? I didn't know about crannogs in those days. Clearly this was once an area of great activity in megalithic times. The tall standing stone outside Achaban proved this. Having grown up with a monolith by the front door, it never occurred to me that this was in any way unusual.

As for the island at the far end of the loch, I discovered the remains of a dry-stone wall which could indeed have once formed a house, and there was evidence of a path but it would only be possible to walk from shore to island in an exceptional drought. Perhaps the water level had risen and this was proof that the climate had once been much warmer – who knows.

Over the next few years, I spent many happy times rowing around the loch. I was sometimes accompanied by friends, or house guests who enjoyed fishing. At other times I lumped the portable Roberts in the boat for company – transistor radios had not been invented. Occasionally I trailed a spinner, although I feared I might catch an evil-looking pike instead of the sweet and tasty little brown trout that inhabited the loch, although this was unlikely since no-one had ever seen a pike in the loch. During the long days of summer there was nothing more agreeable than going out on a warm evening after dinner, knowing it would still be light at ten o'clock. The stillness of the air, the gentle dipping of the oars in the water, the misty haze rising from the surface, the cry of a lone seagull, all contributed to creating an unforgettable experience.

Above all, I made a discovery, like Ratty, that there were few joys greater than just messing about in boats.

CHAPTER THIRTEEN

Mull is a large and varied island with mountains, moorland, lochs and forests, and nowhere is far from the sea. When time for sightseeing was limited, it was possible to complete a round trip in a day, even before the roads were improved, and this would cover most of the island. Starting from the crossroads at Kinloch, we could follow a route forming a figure of eight, avoiding repetition and taking in the central and northern parts of the island.

Although I had now been to Tobermory several times, and to Ballygown to collect Arnish, I had never travelled round the far north of Mull and so, as a special treat for my thirteenth birthday, Puddy offered to take me. I sat in the back of the car as usual while Puddy drove and Margie sat in the passenger seat, talking non-stop with Lottie on her lap. She always had plenty to say, often of a scandalous nature, due to her showbusiness life in London. So she was in her element as we passed the island of Inch Kenneth. A towering cream-coloured building, easily seen from the road, had the appearance of a block of flats and was holiday home to the extraordinary and eccentric Lord and Lady Redesdale. Their six daughters, known collectively as the Mitford Sisters, were famous and notorious in equal measure. Nancy, the eldest, was a popular writer, and Deborah, the youngest, became Duchess of Devonshire, but according to Margie, two of the others, Diana and Unity, brought notoriety to this island by their admiration of the Nazis and friendship with Adolf Hitler. Another sister, Jessica, had Communist leanings, and evidently suggested that Inch Kenneth be used as a Russian submarine base. As a precaution, permits were required for landing on Mull during the war, although that could also have been because of the naval activity in the seas around Mull and the fact that Loch-na-Keal provided a deep water anchorage, which was used as a rendezvous point for Atlantic convoys.

Inch Kenneth was famous historically for the visit in 1773 by Dr Samuel Johnson and James Boswell as guests of Sir Allan Maclean, who lived there with his daughters. Duart Castle was in ruins at the time and it would not be until the early 1900s that Sir Fitzroy Maclean restored this fortress, with its commanding position at the entrance to the Sound of Mull, to a habitable state.

Continuing to the head of Loch-na-Keal, we turned the sharp bend at Knock and over a narrow humpback bridge before passing the pretty little church at Gruline, nestling among the trees. It was the only

Episcopal church on Mull and Puddy and I sometimes went to special services there. Puddy had joined the Anglican church when at school, a fact which Kitten and Grandpop accepted with tolerance if not approval. One Easter my school friend Gilly came with us to church. After the service Puddy arranged to meet friends for drinks in the Salen Hotel nearby but the keys to the bar were missing along with the barman. After several verses of 'why are we waiting?!' he arrived with apologies but without remorse. He attended the Presbyterian kirk across the road where the sermon was even longer than normal. He felt his need to open the bar an insufficient excuse for creeping out before the sermon ended but he was happy to accept a dram in recognition of his devotion to church while not forgetting his duty.

Between Gruline and Salen the short stretch of road, known locally as Melles's Speedway, was unusually broad and straight. According to Margie, a previous owner of the Gruline estate was also a councillor who made sure that his home was linked to Salen by a good road. We continued to Tobermory, admiring the magnificent views up and down the Sound of Mull from the heady heights above Ardnacross. We could see the hills around Loch Sunart in the distance leading to Ardnamurchan, the most westerly point of the British mainland.

After a brief stop in Tobermory, we passed the Mishnish Lochs before a series of steep hairpin bends challenged both car and driver while producing oohs and aahs from the passengers. The neat village of Dervaig was yet to appeal to incomers – those people coming from elsewhere to make a new life in a remote Highland village. Right or wrong, they were perceived by the locals as having a tendency to impose their own ideas upon the place instead of adapting to the customs and ways of the Highlands. In later years Margie told a joke about young ladies from the Home Counties popping out of their front doors and calling 'Anyone for tennis?' How true this was I could never establish, but it countered the disparaging remarks said to be made by people from the north of Mull, who referred to those of us in the south as 'Bog Arabs', thus offending more than one culture.

Further along the road, we reached the white expanse of Calgary Bay, the only sandy beach in the north of Mull and sometimes described as the only one of its kind on Mull, but that was because the people in the north had never seen the wonderful stretches of pristine beaches along the southern coast with which we were familiar. It demonstrated clearly the difference between the two halves of the island – the north made up of large secluded estates, the south of small farms and crofting townships where roads and paths gave access to the coastline.

According to Kitten, her grandmother could remember the boats departing from Mull with their cargo of islanders, destined to endure an Atlantic crossing that would take a month or more to reach Canada. Cleared from the land to make way for sheep runs and deerstalking by a new breed of landowners, some never survived the voyage while others made a success of the opportunities provided by the new land. The story goes that a commissioner in the Canadian Mounted Police spent a summer at Calgary Castle nearby, and upon returning to Canada he suggested the name for Fort Calgary which later became Calgary, Alberta.

From Calgary we followed the road to Ballygown, birthplace of Arnish our goat, and a little further along we stopped to admire Eas Fors waterfall, the tallest on Mull. It was in three sections, the lowest dropping 100 ft directly into the sea. Its name repeated the word 'waterfall' in different languages – Gaelic *Eas*, Norse *Fors*, and then English, demonstrating the diverse cultures who had inhabited Mull, perhaps at the same time, without understanding each other's language.

Across narrow Loch Tuath lay the Isle of Ulva, but it is unlikely that Lord Ullin lost his daughter across this narrow strait. The great romantic poem 'Lord Ullin's Daughter' by Thomas Campbell appealed to me on the same level as Scott's 'Young Lochinvar'. It was not surprising to discover that Campbell knew the area well, while working as a tutor on Mull at a time when a ferry crossed the width of Loch-na-Keal from Gribun to Ulva and that could be wild indeed. Beatrix

Potter was a frequent visitor to the island, where her cousin was married to the laird, and Miss Potter dedicated *The Tale of Mr Tod* to their son. She may not have realised that the population once exceeded six hundred souls although the many ruins provided visual evidence. The Clearance of Ulva was notorious and undertaken with little regard for the people. It could be argued that it was unavoidable. After the collapse of the kelp industry, there was no means of sustaining so many families on impoverished land. The gathering of seaweed provided plenty of work for the islanders, and prosperity for the landowners, over several generations. Seaweed was used as fertiliser on the land, and it was dried and burnt in preparation for export to the mainland where chemical processes were used to manufacture soap and glass. But this industry came to an end when a tax on imported kelp was removed after the Napoleonic Wars. It was a shattering blow to island communities, resulting in abject poverty. The introduction of large sheep runs and deerstalking were seen by some as a means of 'improvement'.

There were ruined buildings all over Mull but it would be wrong to assume these were all the result of the Clearances. Indeed, many cottages which were inhabited in the 1950s are now ruins, having been abandoned in favour of the comforts of putty-coloured kit houses which litter the landscape. To find genuine Clearance villages involves a good map and a trek over rough land, for there were no roads at the time when these were occupied.

Throughout the island we could see patches on the hillside where sunshine exposed undulating parallel ridges, the mis-named lazy beds that once provided depth to the soil and the only means of cultivation on barren land. Potatoes were the main crop, using seaweed as fertiliser to form the mounds. But the potato blight of the mid 1840s caused further distress. Those who were fit enough to survive a voyage to Canada or Australia were perhaps to be envied, but they would never forget their homeland.

It was on the section of the road overlooking Ulva and its empty hills that I celebrated the entry to my teen years in a way which would surely now meet with disapproval. Puddy pulled the car over to admire the view and Margie, a keen smoker, reached for a cigarette and snapped open her lighter. On a whim, Puddy seized the packet and offered me a cigarette. Surprised by this sudden advancement to adult life, I readily accepted the offer and lit up. I drew on the cigarette with a deep intake of breath and a few moments of convulsive coughing and spluttering quickly convinced me that I was not prepared to suffer discomfort for the sake of sophistication. From then on I reserved cigarettes purely for use as a midge repellent. But a word of warning: this strategy does not always work.

The rest of the road followed the coastline to meet the crossroads at Gruline. We had completed the northern circuit of Mull and we now had the choice of returning through Glen More, or by the Gribun Rocks. In those days, before the Glen road was improved, we had no hesitation. Although we could have avoided repeating the same road by going through the Glen, the Gribun route, while narrow and twisting, took less time and was more pleasant despite the risk of being hit by falling rocks.

Some of the most beautiful places on Mull are off the beaten track and one of our favourite spots was Carsaig, although it was not for the faint-hearted. The road south from Pennyghael passed through a lonely glen before reaching a deep cutting with a narrow gorge on the right and dramatic cliffs beyond. There came a moment when the road reached an abyss – with the prospect of being launched into the air and consequent abrupt drop into the sea. Once more I was in the back of Florrie on a sightseeing trip when we reached this point and, without any warning, Margie leapt out of the car, yelling instructions for Puddy to carry on without her, so leaving us to our fate. Had we been going more than twenty miles an hour, we might have taken off, but of course we didn't and Margie returned to the car a few moments later, looking a trifle sheepish. It was a lucky thing she never learnt to drive.

Carsaig was a favourite place for a long walk. After parking Florrie near the old pier, there was a choice of direction – to follow a path on the left which led to Lochbuie, or pass in front of the two large houses on the right. Over the years Puddy brought me and a succession of school friends with the aim of reaching the famous Carsaig Arches. The path was not easy to follow, for the whole coastline was strewn with rocks of every size, shape and form: some like giant sponges, others like Gruyère cheese. In among the rocks were all manner of flotsam and jetsam from old fishing floats to complete ships' masts. Inevitably these raised questions to which we could only surmise the answer and our collective imagination ran riot. We encountered at least one evil-looking mine, the sort we had only ever seen in war films, a ball covered in spikes that we did not dare touch. And every so often we found the skull of a goat with long curved horns, its body a mangled heap among the rocks. It was another reminder of the Clearances. The goats may have been introduced by the Vikings, but were now feral, abandoned when the people left the land. They clung to a perilous existence on the ledges of these great cliffs and sometimes apparently lost their footing.

We never did reach the Arches, but we did stop to examine the carved crosses on the walls of the Nun's Cave. This great cave was said to have been a refuge for the nuns dismissed from Iona by St Columba. He famously said, 'Where there is a cow, there is a woman, and where there is a woman, there is mischief.' But it is more likely that the nuns came here at the time of the Reformation.

The first time we did this walk it was with my friends

Liz and Di, and it took much longer than we expected so Puddy thought we should ring Achaban to explain why we were so late. On our way home, she stopped the car halfway up the hill and made the call at the telephone box near a waterfall. This telephone box was already famous. It featured in the film *I Know Where I'm Going!* made in 1945. Much of the action took place at Carsaig but, although it was a love story, the actor who played the male lead, Roger Livesey, never went to Mull. He was in a London play at the time, and all his scenes were shot in a studio while a double was used in long shots on location. More recently the same red telephone box appeared in *Entrapment* starring Sean Connery and Catherine Zeta-Jones, and it is still there.

I sat with my friends in the car while Puddy made her call, but she was out in a few moments. 'We must hurry home,' she said. 'Jimmy-the-Missionary has brought three young men to see you!' And hurry we did – raising the speed from twenty to thirty miles an hour all the way home. Sure enough, Jimmy-the-Missionary, who once supplied a choir from the Iona Community to help raise funds for a new village hall, was with a group of cadets from Dartmouth Naval College. He brought them to Achaban on the off-chance that we would be home. As soon as we arrived back, we hurriedly cleaned ourselves up before presenting ourselves. It was rare to meet young men, so to find three at once was too good a chance to miss. They were indeed delightful and they invited us to a dance in

Iona the following day, but Di and Liz were leaving, so I went to Iona on my own and stayed in the Rome Express. I had the young cadets all to myself and kept in touch with them for some years to come.

One day Johnnie-the-Postman delivered a large white envelope addressed to Puddy. It contained a crisp invitation with engraved lettering and, to my surprise, it included me. It was an invitation from John's regiment to a garden party at Stirling Castle. Being thirteen had become rather special. Puddy immediately ordered material and set to work, cross-legged on the floor, with her old Singer sewing machine. She soon made a pretty dress for me, and asked Margie to choose a hat to go with it which duly arrived in the post. Puddy and I set off for Stirling with our finery and we stayed at the Golden Lion Hotel, where I was highly impressed by the shiny new plum-coloured ceramic fittings in the ladies' powder room, setting a trend for the ubiquitous avocado suites that would transform bathrooms up and down the country. This was the grand life indeed. Unfortunately, as we must have expected, the Scottish summer failed to favour the garden party and rain forced the event indoors to the Officers' Mess in the Old Palace of James IV. It didn't matter. The officers, including John, wore their kilts, and their shiny silver buttons, the elegant candlesticks and displays of trophies added up to a glittering and memorable occasion. Then the rain eased off so we strolled through the gardens, filled with the fresh smell of roses, and walked round the walls with stunning views of the Wallace Monument, and the hills of the Highlands in the distance.

So it was that a garden party in the Officers' Mess at Stirling Castle, rather than the lure of smoking, elevated me towards adult life.

CHAPTER FOURTEEN

Most people in Mull would agree that the question most frequently asked is: 'What do you find to do here?' As though isolation was synonymous with a vacuum that has to be filled. It is quite possible to sit back and do nothing without feeling too ashamed about it. But the fact is that we never had time on our hands. There was always plenty to do in or around the house.

The long summer days could extend late into the evening, with a rosy glow in the northern sky well past midnight. In winter we gladly drew the curtains, lit the lamps, and settled down to keep warm in front of the fire. Both Kitten and Margie were keen knitters, producing magnificent shawls so fine they could pass through a wedding ring, or chunky jumpers well suited to bitter weather. Puddy was good at knocking up clothes of all sorts, not just for garden parties, on her old Singer sewing machine. She sat cross-legged on the floor, turning the wheel with one hand while carefully guiding the material with the other. If all went well, she could be wearing a new dress the next day, but sometimes the machine snarled up and she had to try a drop of oil to loosen it. One evening, in the depth of winter, the machine stopped working and all her effort to release the snag went to nothing. She needed the dress for a special occasion and all she could do was offer a little prayer. Within a few moments, she heard knocking on the front door and, being a dark night, in the middle of nowhere, she was a little reluctant to see who was there. You can imagine her astonishment when she discovered a Singer salesman on the doorstep! He was well equipped with tools in his van and soon had the sewing machine running smoothly again. She finished the dress without further delay and was both grateful and surprised by the power of prayer. I have her machine to this day, and it still works, but I don't squat on the floor to use it.

Puddy also invested in a large hand loom which required a lot of space. She erected it in the cottage where the sound of its clacking would disturb no-one. Despite her complete lack of experience in the craft of weaving, she had ambitious plans to produce tartan travel rugs and shawls that would be light and easy to post as presents to friends and family. It was never to be a commercial enterprise, but it was a serious occupation. She studied the intricate designs of the setts that made each tartan distinctive, and spent many hours setting up the warp, threading each strand through the eye of the heddle. The light of oil lamps did not make this an easy task and I sometimes helped her, but the weaving part was much more fun, when the pattern gradually emerged in all its vibrant colour. Puddy made several of these beautiful rugs and shawls, which came in handy as wedding presents, but one of them she kept, and I have it still.

When Puddy wasn't making or mending, she was writing, in pencil, in longhand, on plain sheets of paper, on a clipboard with a chunky India rubber attached by a string. Long before she collaborated with Nicholas she acquired a literary agent, but the severe post-war paper shortage reduced her chances of publication. It was not until many years later that she finally succeeded when an early novel, A Breeze in the Barley, became the first part of a trilogy called Kilcaraig, published in 1982.

After dinner we usually sat in the drawing-room. Grandpop would sit on one side of the fireplace, chuckling over his favourite column in The Scotsman, while Kitten sat bolt upright on the other side, reading stories in Gaelic. This did not come easily to her, although she spoke Gaelic fluently. She had been educated at the little school up the road at a time when children were chastised for speaking the language they spoke at home. As a result, she learnt to read and write in English. She was able to read Gaelic but always had difficulty writing it. Like many islanders of her time, she was scathing towards those who tried to learn Gaelic, and was the first to notice their shortcomings. Also, Gaelic varies from island to island and she claimed that the Mull Gaelic was superior to any other.

She could have been right. It was, after all, from the monks in Iona that its influence spread.

When the whole family was at home we sometimes played Monopoly round the dining-room table, with John acting as banker – and act he did, putting on a silly voice which made us all laugh. Or we played Scrabble, a new game that we renamed Squabble because it invariably resulted in arguments about whether a certain word was allowable.

As another diversion, we watched home movies. John had been given a Kodak 8 cine camera as a boy and he had taken it to India when he visited his parents, Kitten and Grandpop, shortly before the war. They were always talking about their time there, so I loved watching the short, flickering reels of film projected onto the dining-room wall. It was one of the few times when the electric-lighting plant was used to power the projector and not just for pumping water.

Nicholas gave a detailed description of the concert he attended at the school, when Jimmy-the-Missionary, who had introduced us to the Dartmouth Cadets, gathered a choir from the Iona Community. Other events took place there and one of the most memorable was the reception that followed a double wedding at the little church by the loch. Imagine sharing your special day as a bride with another! I think they were sisters, and the day of their wedding was not only dry but sunny. After the ceremony, a piper led the two couples the short distance from the church to the school where long trestle tables had been arranged to form a horse-shoe shape. And then a huge sit-down meal was served. It was a very special occasion.

Sundays were different from other days of the week: no ferries, no shops, no washing on the line, and no playing – at least in public. One day, as a small girl, using a little walking stick which Grandpop had fashioned for me, I took it into my head to walk across the Big Park. Stooping and limping, I tried to emulate poor old John Maclean as he delivered the milk. I was soon in big trouble. I had been seen from the scullery window and received a severe reprimand, not because I mimicked poor old John Maclean, but because it was Sunday. Even at a tender age I inwardly questioned this logic but I took it to heart that on 'Sunday, Sunday, Sabbath Day, little children should not play, run about or make a noise like the naughty girls and boys'.

Kitten loved to play the piano, strumming 'Scotland the Brave' with her crumpled hands, and teaching me Gaelic songs, but not on Sundays. And the service, at three o'clock, prevented us from sleeping off Sunday lunch.

One Sunday, a school friend was staying who had not packed a hat. We kept a selection of spare hats in the cloakroom, but she was unimpressed by the choice, so I agreed to go to church uncovered to keep her company. Whether by choice or chance, the minister's sermon centred on St Paul's Letter to the Corinthians exhorting women to cover their heads. We could not escape his eyes in the sparse and scattered congregation so had no option but to sit stoically while he developed his theme for a full thirty minutes. It would be many years before I ventured into a church service without a hat.

Kitten often hosted ceilidhs in the drawing-room – although never on a Sunday, of course. We sang to the accompaniment of the piano or listened to mystical stories told by Hughie Lamont, a man of many talents, who spoke English with the melodious cadence of a true Gael. Hughie also played the pipes and sang at the concerts in Bunessan, five miles away. It had its own village hall in addition to its school. The concerts were advertised to start at eight o'clock and the long wooden benches soon filled up with people who had come from near and far. Some of the participants liked to fortify their courage with a wee dram or two followed by a chaser of beer which was available at the inn nearby, but closing time was nine o'clock. This caused some delays in the concert programme, which could last well into the night.

The concert always started with a medley of pipe tunes played by Calum, or Hughie and his brother Duncan, while the audience tapped the beat with their feet. A Gaelic song followed, often many verses long, with a chorus that everyone sang, even if they didn't speak Gaelic, and didn't know the meaning of the words. They could be fairly sure that the theme was gloomy – of dying chiefs, lost lovers, parting boats.

One of the principal performers was Jeannie Gibson. Jeannie was a wee woman with enormous pluck. She always wore her best clothes to sing in the concerts – her dark trouser-suited postie's uniform. Every day, whatever the weather, she walked up to thirteen miles across country, carrying the post, delivering to houses far from any road. She did not start work until the post arrived on the mail bus late in the afternoon, so during the day she ran her crofts – three of them, with cattle, sheep, and a Highland pony. That is how Puddy came to know her and I once went with Puddy to visit her in the tiny cottage where she lived with her aunt. Jeannie became clerk to her crofting township – a cluster of crofts in Ardtun, near Bunessan, and for her services to agriculture on Mull she was rewarded a well-deserved MBE. Her repertoire included some of the oldest Gaelic songs, and tears often sprang to the eyes upon hearing her crooning presentation.

Some light relief followed with an accordion duet which soon set the feet tapping again. The evening continued in this vein until the interval when cups of tea made a welcome break before the programme resumed and the whole process was repeated. During the evening, the Tilley lamps that burned so brightly at the start of the concert gradually dimmed, their constant hiss sending the audience into a soporific daze, but a brief pumping action on each lamp soon alerted everyone before the final acts in the concert. A dance always followed, but we usually withdrew discreetly before it started.

CHAPTER FOURTEEN

Bunessan village hall was also the venue for film shows provided by the Highlands and Islands Film Institute which toured the area with a little van carrying a generator, screen, and projector. The programme usually included cowboys and Indians or Laurel and Hardy accompanied by yells of delight from the audience, but the most popular films had local themes, so *I Know Where I'm Going!* and *Whisky Galore!* could not fail to please. The novelty of seeing a film presentation was somewhat offset by the quality of the experience. The black and white movies tended to crackle and pop, and on occasion stick altogether, resulting in a small white blotch spreading to all corners of the screen – a true white-out caused by the lamp in the projector burning a hole in the film. Also, there were frequent intervals while each reel of film was changed, and on one occasion the projector failed halfway through so we went home early and never did find out what happened.

Nicholas gave an excellent account of the annual ploughing match, where all the working horses appeared in their finery and competed against each other. He did not mention the local agricultural show that also took place at Bunessan, up on the hill in the grounds of the school. It was the biggest annual event in the Ross of Mull and its position was stunningly beautiful, looking across the sea towards the great headland of Burg, and Staffa like a ship at anchor, with the Treshnish Isles in the distance. But all eyes were on the pens of patient sheep and cattle, spruced up in preparation for the judges. It was a great social occasion where Gaelic could be heard among the farmers who wore their smartest tweeds for the event.

Sometimes we contributed to the domestic section which was displayed within the school building. One year Puddy was in a baking mood and she made a chocolate cake covered with white icing. This formed the background to the artwork that followed. Using one of my little paintbrushes, and several different edible colourings, she painted a depiction of the show, complete with Highland cows, sheep, and collie dogs. It was worthy of exhibition in the Tate Gallery and she was not surprised when a large red card proclaimed it first prize in the Fancy Cake class. Nevertheless, she wanted to preen herself in front of her cake and asked me to join her. As we stood and looked at it with swelling pride, a woman passed behind us and said to her friend, 'I think that cake looks disgusting!' – which just goes to show how careful one should be when passing judgement in public.

The largest show in Mull took place in a field near Salen where sheep, cattle, and a few ponies gathered from all over the island. It was too far to take Corrie but Puddy once entered Carla in the Fancy Dog section. First prize went to a dog with very obscure parentage so Puddy decided never to subject Carla to that humiliation again.

Nicholas could not hide his disappointment that

his dearest friend, Corrie, won third prize when she competed at the Royal Highland Show, but he need not have worried. Her beauty wooed the judges the following year when she won first prize in her class. And to top that, at the age of five, her foal (called Annabel) was declared Highland pony champion of the show in 1959, so honour was truly satisfied.

Reports of the local shows and sales of work appeared in the *Oban Times* a week or so later. The paper was published on Thursdays and came in the post, along with the daily papers, letters and parcels. The coming of the post was a high point of the day. The mail bus passed the house in the late afternoon on its way to the Post Office where Betty-and-her-Mother sorted it ready for Johnnie-the-Postman. Carla took up her position on the old oak chest in front of the dining-room window an hour or so in advance of his arrival. As Nicholas recorded, we never knew what plans she had in mind, if any, and we didn't want to find out, so we kept the door firmly shut.

As a small girl I joined Kitten upstairs in her bedroom where the big bay window gave a good view of the road. I sat on a pouffe at her feet while she knitted intricate Shetland shawls and told stories of the days when she was a young girl growing up in the district. With the art of a true Celt, she interlaced her tales with reports of her encounters with the fairies of the loch. She had the magical power to stretch my belief and I was enthralled. I encouraged her to recite the same tales over and over again, which she did, often accompanying her accounts with a graceful and mysterious dance. She called it the Fairy Dance, but I realised in later years that it owed more to Isadora Duncan and 'health and beauty' than to the fairies at the end of the loch. If only I had absorbed her stories, or taken notes, but I did not. Despite being fascinated, I dismissed the memories of an unusual, even pioneering lifetime, as the maunderings of a loveable old lady and consigned the true stories, along with the false, to the land of the fairies.

As Kitten and I sat in the bay window, watching the road, we were never disappointed. Whatever the weather – sunshine, storm or snow – the stooped shape of Johnnie-the-Postman could be relied upon to appear over the brow of the hill, pedalling his bicycle with a steady, measured pace. Speedy he was not – indeed we marvelled at his ability to keep upright while moving so slowly, even downhill. Leaving his bicycle by the gate, he struggled to extract our mail from a bag bloated with letters, papers and parcels for the scattered cottages throughout the district. Sometimes we asked him to dispatch some luckless hen, waiting in the box at the gate. More often we were simply relieved that, once again, we had kept him apart from Carla who was a frenzy of barking and gnashing teeth on the other side of the dining-room door.

The letters and daily newspapers kept us in touch with events in the world around us – events that seldom affected us directly, but might make history. So it was disturbing when world history came a little too close for comfort. The Suez Crisis became headline news in 1956 and we listened to each bulletin with growing concern. We soon learnt that John's regiment was to be sent to the war zone and we were not the only family on Mull to be affected. Other Mull men belonged to the regiment and the colonel lived in Tobermory. His wife wanted to be with him at the depot to prepare for the regiment's departure but she could not take their children with her, so a pair of twins and their big sister came to stay at Achaban. They brought a load of toys with them, but my abiding memory is of their fascination with our cuckoo clock. John had brought it home from Germany, where he had been stationed with the regiment, and it hung on the kitchen wall. The twins spent fifteen minutes of every hour standing in front of the clock, waiting for the cuckoo to pop out of his house to announce the hour. They were never disappointed.

Nicholas was wise to refrain from political comment. Plenty enough has been written about the Suez Crisis since it turned out to be something of a debacle. We were just thankful to know that the regiment would soon be on its way home.

Chapter Fifteen

From Achaban it really wasn't necessary to use a car as there were places to explore in all directions, on foot, bicycle or even dog cart. Nicholas wrote about the granite quarry at Tormore, and there was no doubt that this was one of our favourite walks for it could be short or long, depending on how energetic or inquisitive we felt. The path to Tormore passed the burial ground and Fionnphort House, a solid granite building with a slate roof. It was of one storey, and was Kitten's birthplace, but by the 1950s it had become home to the ferrymen before it burnt down and was replaced by a modern ferry house. The fine granite from old Fionnphort House was fittingly shipped to Iona for use in the restoration of the Abbey buildings.

A rough path led to the top of the quarry where great blocks of the distinctive pink granite were still in place, piled high ready for shipment, but demand declined long before the First World War and the quarry closed. Much of the equipment lay abandoned, including the rails which were used to transfer the granite blocks to the pier. From the sandy beach we liked to scramble up the bank to Dead Man's Cave, with its tiny window beside the low entrance. It was believed that bodies destined for burial in Iona were kept there overnight. Sometimes we walked back up the steep hill, or scrambled round by the shore, depending on the state of the tide. The view from the top of the quarry was unsurpassed, taking in the range of colours represented by rock, sea, sand and grass. It was a combination of natural tones that could not be rivalled anywhere on earth.

Looking south, the wide panorama included the back of Achaban and the loch. To the right, the village of Fionnphort straggled down towards the jetty and, in the background, a road led towards the Isle of Erraid. Puddy and I often followed this road, taking turns to ride Corrie. She was the most patient, easy-going pony, but there was one stretch of the road which seemed to spook her. It passed through a narrow passage between walls of solid rock. She would throw back her ears, pull her chin into her chest and swing round in circles before we could entice her to move forward. Once past these great rocks, she was her normal calm self again. Puddy was convinced that there must be a good reason and found an old map which indicated the site of a burial ground nearby. Could it be that Corrie sensed this? We could never know.

Beyond a narrow bridge, and a ford, the road led to the beautiful white sands of Fidden, but a turn to the left near old Fidden farm followed a track to

Knockvologan where a narrow path dropped down towards a secluded beach opposite Erraid. This track passed a little whitewashed cottage with a thatched roof and a wooden chimney stack at one end set at a rakish angle. It was like many cottages that survived into the early 1900s, often described as black houses. Typically a black house did not have a chimney, but a central hearth, allowing the smoke to filter through the heather thatch. This was superior, and was the last remaining inhabited cottage of its kind in Mull. It was home to old Mary Cameron who lived alone. She regularly walked to the Post Office in Fionnphort to buy her messages which she carried home in a canvas haversack on her back. She smiled and nodded by way of communication, for her English was limited. She would refuse all offers of a lift home in the car, but she was happy to accept on behalf of her haversack.

Old Mary Cameron was one of many people of greatly advanced years who lived in the district. Kitten was a mere youngster by comparison. There was one very old lady who lived in a little granite cottage near the Post Office. Her name was Rosina, and she was reputed to be close to a hundred years old. Her cottage was near the road but hidden from view by a high hedge and it had an air of mystery about it. I never saw her, for she seldom came outside, and I was a trifle apprehensive lest she should suddenly appear, conjuring in my mind a haggard apparition lacking flesh and blood. Kitten knew her well, and sometimes expressed a desire to call on her, so Grandpop would drive her down to the village and leave the two old ladies to chat for an hour or so. It gave Kitten a chance to exchange memories of the old days in Gaelic, the language they both understood.

In due course, Rosina joined her folk in the burial ground. The hedge was cut down and the cottage spruced up. With a wooden addition, it became the Keel Row, providing the only bar and restaurant in Fionnphort.

Kitten was not the only one who liked to keep in touch with friends in the district. Puddy was a keen member of the SWRI – or Scottish Women's Rural Institute, to give it its full title. She walked to the meetings which took place in the little school and picked up ideas from visiting speakers, watched demonstrations of flower arranging, or took part in whist or beetle drives.

Our closest neighbour was the schoolteacher who lived opposite the school. She made good use of the long school holidays by travelling to distant places and always had plenty to report, and photographs to show. Puddy arranged to see her in the evening and sometimes I went with her. I listened to their conversation, assuming a look of interest while eyeing a trolley in the corner which remained covered in a cloth. It would not be till late in the evening that the tea cups, saucers and little plates would be revealed. It was the tradition to offer tea accompanied by a range of tempting goodies – scones with jam, and Victoria sponge cake – just when it seemed time to go home. After gorging ourselves on this feast, we walked home by torch light unless there was a full moon, or a clear night sky revealed the astonishing Milky Way spread in all directions, sparkling like crystals encrusted on a wedding veil.

The road beyond the school passed the house where Kaya and his family lived. Puddy could always depend on Kaya for his help, being able to put his hand to so many trades. But his skills as a blacksmith were of greatest use to Puddy, who asked him to trim Corrie's hooves when necessary. Corrie did not need to wear shoes because her hooves were strong and she always walked on soft surfaces, but it was comforting to know that Kaya was close at hand.

Further along, the road came to a cluster of thatched cottages where ducks, hens and geese paid little attention to passing cars, but a collie dog lay in waiting, ready to snap at the wheels. This was Bogilee where Old Charlie lived with his sisters, and ran a small shop. He was called Charlie Bogilee, using his place name, a common practice where so many shared the same surname, and often retained even after they went to live elsewhere. Charlie was always cheerful, a tuft of silver hair capping his round pink face, but he could not move without the aid of sticks. He had lost both legs in the mud of Passchendaele. It was Charlie Bogilee who invariably was first to wish us a Good New Year soon after midnight, struggling out of his house to use the telephone box at the end of the road.

During the mid 1950s these little cottages at Bogilee were extended upwards to become two storeys tall, just like the cottage beside the ferry at Fionnphort which had once been a long, low building with whitewashed walls and a thatched roof. Many thatched roofs were replaced by corrugated iron, often painted bright colours, but the roofing of choice would always be slate.

Another walk took us to Camus, passing a row of thatched cottages close to the main road which were then inhabited, but are now in ruin. We left the car near the only petrol pumps between here and Craignure and set off along a footpath across moorland which veered at an angle to pass alongside a handsome stone wall separating the moor from Ardfenaig. The path led to a deep bay where a row of old stone cottages was used as a residential centre by the Iona Community. These cottages once housed quarry workers, the granite in this area being a paler shade of pink than that of Tormore. Over the hill was Market Bay, *Tràigh na Margaidh*, a pink sandy bay which became a favourite retreat of the royal family seeking seclusion for picnics during their annual summer cruise round the Western Isles aboard *Britannia*.

We retraced our steps alongside the Ardfenaig wall, built, Kitten told us, to give work to the people during times of famine. A large family now lived in Ardfenaig but it was once the home of the notorious Factor Mór, or great factor, who had been appointed chamberlain to the Ross of Mull. The Ross was owned by the Dukes of Argyll, and the 8th Duke was acknowledged to be a good man, but John Campbell, the Factor Mór, was already in place when the Duke inherited the land in 1847. He was possibly unaware of the Factor Mór's habit of shuffling people from place to place like cards in a pack. He did not indulge in the worst form of clearance, such as happened in the north of Mull, but there was a hierarchy in which the cottars were among the bottom of the pile, with no leases or rights to land, and they suffered most while the Factor Mór improved his own land, adding fertile fields to his farm at Ardfenaig. A century later the Factor Mór was still referred to in hushed tones.

Kitten often muttered 'never trust a Campbell', despite the fact that her own second name was Campbell. This could be explained by the respect that was given to the 8th Duke – head of the clan Campbell – by her parents. But it was strange that my mother also bore the name Campbell and only recently I followed a clue. One of the daughters of the 8th Duke, Lady Victoria, was an invalid who was well known for her good works, setting up soup kitchens in Tiree to feed the hungry during years of famine. She was also a frequent visitor to Mull and knew Kitten's parents. It was she who advised a pretty dark-haired girl to leave the island and seek a career as a nurse. That young girl was Kitten, who duly left home and trained in

Edinburgh's Castle Terrace to become a Queen's Nurse – a district nurse visiting and caring for the poor in their own homes long before the NHS was created. And so it was that she met a young medical student while attending a patient in Whitehorse Close at the bottom of Edinburgh's Royal Mile, opposite the Palace of Holyroodhouse. It is picturesque now, but it was a slum in the early 1900s, so less romantic than it sounds. Kitten and Grandpop had to extend their courtship for four years, for in those days medical students were not permitted to marry until fully qualified. Without Lady Victoria Campbell's intervention Kitten would never have become a nurse so they might never have met. This would perhaps account for Kitten bestowing upon her second daughter the name she otherwise despised.

Bunessan was the centre of the district, and once supported many small businesses, but it lacked good shops in the 1950s. The main road passed through but we seldom needed to stop. Occasionally local livestock markets took place near the school, the cattle being shipped from the pier to find fresh pastures on the mainland. The sudden acquisition of large bank notes was something to be celebrated, and where better than the Argyll Arms? A spirited evening followed in the bar, resulting in recumbent bodies adorning the pavement the next morning.

Beyond Bunessan, a pleasant walk could follow much of the route taken by Jeannie Gibson when she delivered the post. Taking the road to Ardtun, it passed scattered cottages, and several gates, to reach Knockan, with views across Loch Scridain towards the great headland of Burg. This was a crofting district unlike any other in Mull and little has changed except that in recent years new houses have popped up and old ruins have been restored. The population which was declining throughout the 1950s is now showing signs of recovery.

Close to the junction where this route joins the main road, a monument remembers Mary Macdonald who lived from 1789-1872. She wrote a beautiful Gaelic hymn, '*Leanabh an Aigh*', set to a traditional tune which Kitten's father used when he conducted a Gaelic choir in the district. The melody was called Bunessan, after the village, and the words translated into English as 'Child in a Manger'. This beautiful hymn was sung at Christmas by the Iona Abbey choir and I loved it so much that I introduced it to a carol service at school. During the 1930s, new words were set to the tune and published in the 'Songs of Praise' hymnal as 'Morning has Broken', but it was not until 1972 that Cat Stevens sang a version which brought it to the top of the charts, and international recognition.

Another road led south from Bunessan to some of the most beautiful beaches you could imagine. The sandy bay at Uisken was a favourite, but if we saw another family spreading out a rug and settling down, we drove to Ardalanish which provided a long stretch of breakers washing onto a gently shelving beach. Few people come to Scotland to sunbathe, let alone swim, but with artful timing, there is no more perfect place – and if, like me, you prefer to swim in salt water without cutting your feet on shingle, or tangling in seaweed, then this is the place to be. The secret is to go in the afternoon when both the sun and the tide have been out in the morning. The sun heats the bare sand and this in turn warms the water as it gradually covers the beach on the incoming tide. The result is the gentle swell of warm sea at swimming-pool depth. Pure bliss.

Unfortunately, time, tide and sunshine wait for no man, so this set of conditions is seldom met, making it all the more precious when it does and an unforgettable experience.

CHAPTER SIXTEEN

'Time never stands still,' Nicholas announced in his memoirs before reflecting on the absurdity of stating the obvious. But he was right, however silly it may have seemed. Some things change imperceptibly, others are more dramatic. And so it was towards the end of the 1950s that life on Mull began to catch up with the rest of the world.

Mains electricity finally reached us in 1958, threaded like the telegraph wires, on poles across the island. It was a great feat of engineering for the benefit of such a small community but, inevitably, the fine wires often succumbed to fierce winter gales so we prudently kept our lamps trimmed in preparation for the blackouts. Due to the courage and resourcefulness, in sometimes extreme conditions, of our local hydro-electric engineers, we seldom had to wait long before the electricity supply was restored. There are now few houses on Mull that do not benefit from mains electricity. There is a story, probably apocryphal, which tells of an old lady on Skye who, when asked if she enjoyed the benefits of electricity, replied, 'Och aye – I can now see to light my lamps!'

For us the change from Direct to Alternating Current was gradual although it meant some upheaval caused by the replacement of our electric wiring and sockets. An old refrigerator, brought out of storage, replaced a small dresser in the kitchen. There was no television reception as yet, so that was not an option, but we could now listen to the wireless with the lights on but without interference from the electric generator. Kitten dispensed with her mangle in favour of a spin-drier and bought an electric iron so the old black flat irons became doorstops and bookends.

Mains water, supplied to the district using Grandpop's design, followed soon after. The road came next and not before time. Throughout the 1940s and most of the '50s Argyll was represented by one Member of Parliament whose death in 1958 resulted in a by-election. For the first time in years a flurry of politicians sought the attention of an electorate whose interest in world affairs was far outweighed by island grievances. Meetings were called in the school, inviting candidates to put their views to the community, but only one question persisted: 'What are you going to do about the Glen road?' To which the hapless politician used all his resources to avoid a straight answer. Even the inherently polite islanders were unable to suppress their jeers. It would not be until the early 1960s that funding finally became available, sparked by a generous private donation, for the building of a new pier at Craignure. The subsequent and inevitable increase in traffic would require upgrading to the road.

This work began during a summer of constant sunshine. The road remained single-track but was widened and long sections straightened, smoothing out the sharpest bends, which involved cutting through solid rock in places. Bitumen transformed the rough surface, and rushes no longer swept the underside of vehicles going through the Glen. From a cautious twenty miles an hour, we could now reach a heady forty – and even more on a straight stretch.

The Forestry Commission was responsible for many new plantations on land declared useless for anything else. The growing trees would in years to come dramatically alter the landscape, obliterating familiar views, but supplying steady work for a few able-bodied men. This was important, because young families were of benefit to the whole island. The population of Mull, having topped 10,000 in 1821, was halved in the following fifty years due to the combined horrors of the Clearances and the potato famine. By 1961 it had more than halved again and seemed to be in terminal decline. The little school closed when the roll dwindled below half a dozen, and the pupils were transferred daily by bus to Bunessan. The building was converted for permanent use as the long-awaited and much valued village hall.

It would be a good many years before white-tailed sea eagles and whale-watching revived an interest in the wild outdoors. The resulting influx of tourists would

not have been possible without improved ferry connections to the mainland. The long-awaited pier was
finally built at Craignure in the mid 1960s, a hundred
years after it was first mooted. By that time I was living
in London and, excited by this development after so
many years of speculation, I happened to say to a smart
young man I knew that we were about to have a new
pier on Mull, whereupon he said, 'Who?!'

The pier at Craignure radically changed ferry
arrangements between Mull and the mainland when
the newly built MV *Columba* carried dozens of cars on
each sailing and, in due course, Sunday sailings were
introduced. It was expected that Craignure would
develop as a result of becoming the Mull terminus, but
little changed.

It so happened I travelled on *Columba* within the
first month of her service to Mull. My diary entry for
Saturday 8th August, 1964 is headed 'A Day in a New
Era' and I described *Columba* as a 'huge, luxurious ship
– shiny and smart, broad and tall with magnificent sun
decks and an observation lounge, and the monstrous
all-digesting hydraulic car lift and garage! She is certainly a very magnificent ship and we can be proud of
her.' Compared to the dear *Lochinvar* I was certainly
impressed by her size and facilities. It would be another
thirty years before the new and seemingly vast roll-on-
roll-off ferry MV *Isle of Mull* came into service on the
Oban to Craignure route in 1988 and *Columba* would
be transformed like Cinderella at the ball into the

diminutive but perfectly formed luxury cruise ship *MV Hebridean Princess*. By one of those strange twists and turns of fate which can divert life in unexpected directions, I was back on board, thirty years later, but in a very different capacity. After a series of career changes throughout my life, I was now a tourist guide, and worked aboard *Hebridean Princess* for several seasons. The transformation was so successful that I could not recognise the old *Columba*, 'magnificent' though she was, when I wrote in my diary on Friday 21st October, 1994: 'The ship is truly superb with every comfort and an attentive and cheerful crew.' There was now no evidence of the hydraulic car lift which had so impressed me thirty years before. Not only did I enjoy her comforts and elegance, but I met some delightful people and had the opportunity I never expected of visiting numerous places around the west coast, including many islands, each different from the other. But nowhere could compare with the infinite variety of Mull and, when asked by the guests aboard *Hebridean Princess*, I could honestly say that my favourite view, apart from our beautiful loch, was from Fionnphort across the Sound to Iona.

The picturesque motorboats which plied across the Sound were replaced by a ferry capable of taking vehicles, as well as tourists, to and from Iona. Campaigners against the introduction of this boat were concerned that visitors would bring their cars, so destroying the peace of Iona, but this did not happen, while farmers and permanent residents enjoyed the benefits, allowing them to transfer goods and livestock with comparative ease.

Dr Beeching's cuts brought an end to the convenience of direct trains between Oban and London. The journey became an obstacle course, for not only was it necessary to change trains at Glasgow, but to change stations as well, a situation which persists to the present day. The line between Stirling and Crianlarich was uprooted and became part of the Strathyre Cycle Path. The pretty wooden station in Oban was demolished and replaced by a block of flats, an insignificant brick ticket office and a bland clock tower, while the Station Hotel opposite was renamed the Caledonian.

But I digress, for all these changes took many years, and I need to return to those fading 1950s.

Florrie was in disgrace once more. John had been home on leave and it was time for him to return to Stirling Castle. Puddy was driving, John was in front, and I was sitting in the back as we approached Craignure. Suddenly there was a clunking sound, and it felt as though the bottom had fallen out of the car. We managed to limp, as if on square wheels, to the jetty to unload John, but radical repairs were needed to restore Florrie to the road. 'We need a new car,' said Grandpop, but he wanted a big one like the Humber he owned before the war while Puddy argued that a small car would be more suitable. 'It would use less petrol,' she pointed out, appealing to Grandpop's parsimonious tendency, and a modest little car was duly ordered. It was not the end of Florrie, however. Once she was repaired, John took her to Stirling to live with him at the castle. So she had a new lease of life after twenty years in Mull.

I owed much to the presence of Kitten and Grandpop in my life. When I was very small Grandpop built a traditional doll's house with two rooms up and down. It was painted white with a green roof and Perspex windows framed in red. Kitten filled it with furniture, supplementing a few bought items with hand-made chairs and chests of drawers made from empty matchboxes. One day I decided upon a thorough spring clean and took all the furniture out, spreading it on the floor beside me. I was filled with good intentions, but it was all too much for me. 'It's an awful job for a little girl like me!' I wailed within Kitten's hearing. She came to my aid at once, offering to complete the task while I ran away to find something else to do. In later years she showed me how to make perfect meringues, crisp on the outsides, gloriously gooey within, and meltingly delicious shortbread biscuits, thin, snappy and buttery. She also taught me Gaelic songs and some useful Gaelic phrases. For instance, that loss of dignity when a stray dog follows can be averted by the sharp command 'Truis!' which all dogs understand. They will hesitate briefly, and upon hearing it repeated, they will turn tail and lope off in the other direction. It never fails.

As a small girl I shadowed Grandpop wherever he went, watching him bodge in the workshop, repair punctures, or gut rabbits. He extended the life of his razor blades by honing them with a stropper, a little box containing the blade which he rubbed up and down a string looped round a tap, a process which he patiently demonstrated to my fascination. He taught me to strum 'Polly Wolly Doodle' on the piano and he introduced me to Scott and Kipling, often quoting passages at length. Each spring he declared war on bracken, aiming at their green shoots thrusting from the earth in tight curls which he clipped off with the handle of his walking stick, like a manic golfer driving a ball. It was he who fashioned the little walking stick for me to wield in a similar fashion. So it was sad to see him gradually decline.

Grandpop had been a good driver but he was becoming frail and his reactions were slowing down. One day he drove to Craignure in the new car to meet Margie and Lottie off the boat. They were driving home through the Glen when they met a bus. Grandpop reversed into a passing place but accidentally put his foot on the accelerator instead of the brake, so the car slid abruptly backwards down the grass bank. Luckily there was no ditch and Grandpop and Margie and Lottie were unscathed but somewhat dazed. The first thing they saw was a row of anxious faces peering down from the road – the bus passengers were probably expecting a twisted lump of metal, but instead they all pulled together and hauled the car back on the road. After that, Grandpop seldom drove again.

He may have been frail, but he had not lost his skills as a physician. We knew the local doctor socially but seldom needed to visit the surgery, which was within the tall house overlooking Bunessan Bay. It was approached by a steeply winding footpath which risked bringing on a cardiac arrest for all but the healthiest of patients. For a brief period Grandpop was asked to act as locum for the doctor and Puddy took on the role of driver. He enjoyed this opportunity to be of use to the community and dealt with all the routine visits as the professional he was. One night he received an emergency call which brought him to the bedside of a much loved lady in the village. She was breathless and in considerable distress. Instantly recognising her symptoms, Grandpop performed a procedure known as a pleural tap, draining the build-up of fluid from the lung which was causing the problem. She quickly recovered and Grandpop's reputation soared throughout the Ross of Mull.

Inevitably, age took its toll among the elderly members of the community and Puddy began to represent the family at all the funerals in the Ross. It was unusual for women to appear by the graveside so she was something of a pioneer. It had become a fact, many years before, that the little graveyard in Fionnphort was so full that there was 'standing-room only'. So most funerals took place in ancient burial grounds along bumpy tracks far from the main road. As more took place in winter than summer, and often when it was wet and windy, Puddy dressed for the occasion in long-johns under her skirt which she referred to as her funeral knickers. With all these difficulties in mind, Grandpop had the forethought to claim a small patch of land on the far side of the garden wall to be ours in perpetuity for use as a burial ground.

It was almost inevitable that Grandpop's coffin would be the first to be lowered gently into his chosen plot, which was consecrated on the day of his burial. Kitten stayed in the house with Margie, while Puddy and I, and a gathering of our closest neighbours in their best dark suits, stood by the grave during the short service of committal. No doubt Puddy was wearing her funeral knickers.

It was a rite of passage and it seemed that nothing would ever be the same again.

It so happens that Nicholas had gone before. He had survived all nine of his lives, but owed much to Grandpop who patiently dressed his paws when they were lacerated by snares, who plucked ticks from his body, who always saw to it that an old blanket would keep him warm during cold nights spent in the engine house, and that his milk was topped up. And it was Grandpop who buried him within the garden wall.

Some things were just the same as ever. In spring, the yellow of the whin on the hill; in summer, the trilling song of the lark ascending; in autumn, the bronzed bracken which had survived Grandpop's war; the skeins of geese in a clear winter sky.

The loch formed a constant view from the house, yet paradoxically it was ever-changing. Seagulls clustered in groups on the water, forming flotillas, punctuating the peace with a sudden explosion of raucous cackles, disputing ownership of some morsel. Clear skies could be transformed in a flash by scudding clouds on a restless wind. They cast their shadows over the low hills around the loch, but at intervals, shafts of sunlight pierced the clouds, highlighting the subtle and varying shades of bracken, heather and stunted trees on the banks. At times the water was grey and angry: the white stripes of foam a sign of worse to come. High winds swept veils of rain across the loch, concealing the far island from view. Within minutes, this could give way to sunshine, glittering like sequins on the water, reflecting sparkles and shimmers. All this could happen within a single day.

But on the best of days, few words could do justice to the scene. So I'll leave the last words to Nicholas, who wrote that 'the loch could be blue, so blue, that to paint it would seem like a coloured lie'.